T0194088

THE KILLING
of THE CHRISTIAN CHURCH
in AMERICA

GENE JACKSON

Order this book online at www.trafford.com
or email orders@trafford.com

Most Trafford titles are also available at major online book retailers.

Print information available on the last page.

ISBN: 978-1-6987-0012-0 (sc)
ISBN: 978-1-6987-0011-3 (hc)
ISBN: 978-1-6987-0013-7 (e)

Library of Congress Control Number: 2020904610

Trafford rev. 03/20/2020

www.trafford.com
North America & international
toll-free: 1 888 232 4444 (USA & Canada)
fax: 812 355 4082

This book is dedicated to incarcerated men who love Jesus. And to volunteers who share the message of Jesus with those who are behind razor-sharp fences and walls.

A special thanks to the one who requested to remain anonymous. His innumerable thoughts, comments, and criticisms were invaluable.

CONTENTS

Introduction xiii

Chapter 1   A Little More About This Writing 1

Chapter 2   What's Happening 3

Chapter 3   Movements and Their Impact 6

Chapter 4   Ways to Evaluate Your Church 9

Chapter 5   The Old Testament 15

Chapter 6   Christianity's Beginning 18

Chapter 7   Centuries of Christianity 26

Chapter 8   Defining Believers and Unbelievers 31

Chapter 9   Noticeables and Unnoticeables 35

Chapter 10 Research: Gather, Sift, Evaluate 44

Chapter 11 Cults and Religious Groups 51

Chapter 12 The Peoples Temple 55

Chapter 13 The Church of Jesus Christ of Latter-Day
Saints (LDS) 58

Chapter 14 Jehovah's Witnesses 68

Chapter 15 Bible-Believing Christian Denominations 76

Chapter 16 The Roman Catholic Church 79

Chapter 17 Southern Baptist Convention Churches (SBC) 87

Chapter 18 United Methodist Church (UMC) 94

Chapter 19 Megachurches 100

Chapter 20 Tele-Evangelists 105

Chapter 21 Modern Day Churches and Ministers 114

Chapter 22 Soupy Ingredients Within Churches................. 119

Chapter 23 My Calling... 123

Chapter 24 Politics within The Church 128

Chapter 25 Defining Titles.. 133

Chapter 26 Being Judgmental of Preachers 140

Chapter 27 A Touchy Subject About Ministers.................... 146

Chapter 28 Church Leaders.. 154

Chapter 29 Teachers... 162

Chapter 30 Faith or Unbelief... 165

Chapter 31 Institutions of Higher Learning......................... 170

Chapter 32 Millennials... 178

Chapter 33 The Media 183

Chapter 34 Lesbians and Homosexuals in The Pulpits 192

Chapter 35 Racism.. 201

Chapter 36 Two Ordinances 208

Chapter 37 The Church within The Community 216

Chapter 38 Christian Lifestyles.. 222

Chapter 39 A Survey of Biblical Knowledge........................ 227

Chapter 40 What God Has Said to His People..................... 232

Conclusion... 239

INTRODUCTION

THE KILLING OF THE CHRISTIAN CHURCH IN AMERICA is closer than one can imagine and is probably unimaginable by multitudes. There are many causes, reasons and trends for the declining failure of churches throughout America. These causes, reasons and trends are contributors for the eventual closing of all Christian churches in America. Many church buildings will remain standing but will not be Christian. Some of these contributors will be examined and discussed in this current project.

Some contents of this book will be considered as fictional by some. But, by the writer, they are prophetic.

When Jesus said, "the gates of hell will not prevail against my church," he was not speaking of buildings made of brick, stone and mortar. But, of followers who would profess faith in Him.

Will all brick and mortar churches go out of business? This will never happen in America will be the thoughts of some. Will it happen over a period-of-time to some churches or all churches? Only the Lord God knows these answers.

When a blood vessel or an artery in a person's body is punctured or penetrated, there will occur blood loss. When nothing is done to stop the bleeding and the loss of blood, death is imminent. When the blood of Jesus is no longer being preached within the church, the church becomes spiritually dead. The failure to preach Jesus is one of the causes in the decline of churches in America.

Thousands of churches are shuttering their doors. Many ministers who previously pastored Christian churches have turned to atheism, joining atheist groups for the purpose of fellowshipping.

Unbelievers, of which there are many within churches, will remain in the same brick and mortar buildings, socializing, fellowshipping, and continuing to call themselves Christians. The churches which remain will be clubs or fellowship gatherings, encouraging social deeds, a prosperity-type ministry and a social gospel of loving your neighbor.

Christianity will not be dead, but still alive in the hearts of believers outside the walls of a building. This is the invisible church which Jesus talked with his disciples about building. Today, many believers, because churches are not preaching the gospel, have given up on church and are practicing their Christianity in other venues. Elijah, an Old Testament prophet, believed that he was the only prophet of God remaining. Christians outside a church building, will be thinking the same thing.

> "and the word of the Lord came to him: 'What are you doing here, Elijah?' He replied, 'I have been very zealous for the Lord God Almighty. The Israelites have rejected your covenant, torn down your altars, and put your prophets to death with the sword. I am the only one left, and now they are trying to kill me too'" (1 Kings 19: 9b-10).

The pace of church closings has begun to quicken. Church attendance has been on the decline for years. Christianity is under attack and on the defensive. Many churches which claim to be Christian…aren't Christian. Some religious groups claim they are Jesus led, but are social and fellowship-oriented cults… preaching a modified version of the Holy Bible. These churches are manmade institutions not led by the Holy Spirit of God.

In one church recently on a Sunday morning, a visiting minister from a well-known Baptist seminary made this statement: "Eighty percent of churches are dying." Perhaps he was speaking of churches in his denomination. Whether he was speaking about his denomination or not: churches in all denominations are decaying. The elderly fade into the sunset while untold millions of millennials are adapting and adopting today's ungodly cultural teachings. Due to the absence of the millennials to replace the elderly, churches close.

Listening to the visiting professor, I knew that he was wrong. Perhaps, not about the eighty percent, for it could be more-or-less. What wasn't said was that some churches were already dead and didn't know it. He said that they were dying. Thousands of churches are already dead spiritually. Yes, dead already, not knowing it, but still in existence.

This book is about physical churches where believers and unbelievers are mingling together. Believers, who are trying to live the faith, but who have very limited knowledge of the Holy Bible. Then, there are unbelievers in all churches and denominations, who are in the church for varying reasons.

The purpose of this book is to present insights into the causes, reasons and trends why churches are not only closing now, but over coming years will completely lose their Christian influence. God is involved in these closings. God is longsuffering but will not continue to be patient with those who continue to misuse His Name. God has a timeframe for everything.

This writing will give insights to the reader as to when, whether in your generation or in the next, there will be a sign on your church's lawn or on its door with the words "Church for Sale."

The reader should not consider this book to be a negative one. Its purpose is informative so the churchgoing public will take off their rose-colored glasses and consider the negative infiltrating causes, reasons and trends taking place within their church. Negativism is not an issue.

Whether subjectivity or objectivity is displayed by my presentations of these trends, only the reader can decide. It's not written to convince or persuade. My effort is merely to present some facts.

As Sergeant Joe Friday would say, *"Just the facts, ma'am."*

author

CHAPTER ONE

A LITTLE MORE ABOUT THIS WRITING

READING SOME OF BILL O'REILLY'S BOOKS, I QUESTION why he has not written about what is killing Christian churches in America. Perhaps it's because all churches in America are not totally dead or conflict with his beliefs. Mr. O'Reilly's book titles include many killings: Lincoln; Kennedy; Patton; the SS; England; Reagan; Rising Sun; and Jesus. His books don't need any promoting from me, since they are well written and read by millions.

The inspiration for writing this book didn't come from any of Mr. O'Reilly's books, but has come directly from my belief that it's time to write about the causes, reasons and trends causing the decline and eventual killing of Christian churches in America. During the past sixty-five years, churches in America have been on a rollercoaster ride downward.

"THE KILLING OF THE CHRISTIAN CHURCH IN AMERICA" is to acquaint Christians and society with the fact that today's Christianity in America has no similarity to what was being preached in the first century by the apostles and disciples. It should be obvious to church attendees, especially true believers, that churches which they are attending are not only dying, but some are already dead.

Christianity started off in the first century on a Boeing 737 Airliner, having layovers over the centuries, and then hopped onto a Piper Cub in the twenty-first century. The Christian mission to evangelize and win disciples has become

1

slower, exhausted, and out of breath. While the population growth is explosive, Christianity is unable to keep pace.

✢ EMPTY STRUCTURES

Churches are daily closing their doors in rural areas, suburbs, towns, and cities. Empty church buildings dot the landscape throughout the USA. Sale signs in front of many of these empty structures aren't present. Some denominations, and those who once sat in their now empty pews, don't know what to do with these buildings.

Former members won't be able to personally profit from the sale of any of these properties. Churches are non-profit religiously organized and tax-free institutions. The profit from any sales may be used to pay off debts, go to the denomination or will be left for lawyers and government regulators to decide.

Some churches with closed doors will be turned over to other nationalities or immigrants who have set up residence in the USA. Some churches, especially those in rural area which have cemeteries, will remain unused, empty and dilapidated.

In heavily populated areas of African Americans, some former Caucasian churches will be sold or donated to these bodies.

Some older buildings will be taken over by the Historical Society and could become museums and arts centers.

CHAPTER TWO

WHAT'S HAPPENING

✧ TODAY'S MODERN CHRISTIANITY

CHURCHES SHOULD HAVE SIMILARITIES TO THOSE OF the first century. The message being preached today should be the same as the one which the early church preached. Christians are now living in a cultural and politically correct society divorced from the teachings of God. Over the centuries, modifications to the Holy Bible have been made by denominations.

It is difficult to identify Christians in the workplace, and sometimes even in the pews of a church. Multitudes of Christians today don't believe in professing their faith. If a person had to choose between two people sitting side-by-side in a workplace as to which one is Christian and which one isn't, it would be as difficult as choosing which hand the pea is in.

Tom Brokaw coined the words, *'The Greatest Generation'* when referring to the World War II era. The greatest generation for Christianity occurred during the first century when Christians went throughout the known world spreading the good news about Jesus Christ. This ignited flames which existed in the hearts of early Christians and spread for centuries throughout the Roman Empire. What was known to the Romans as a movement of *"The Way"* was viewed as a cult and not an approved religion. It took centuries for Christianity to be an approved recognized religion by the Romans. Christianity was first viewed as a Jewish sect.

Tom Brokaw's *"Greatest Generation"* were men and women who had survived the great depression of the 1930s and had left home and families to fight in World War II. This generation was the families who lived on farms, worked in mills and factories, moved to the cities for jobs, and had very little or no wealth to show for their efforts. They were dependent on God for their deliverance from poverty and from a death on a battlefield in a foreign country. Untold sacrifices were made by millions.

Mothers put stars in their window for sons and daughters whom they had not seen for years who were now in foreign lands fighting for freedom. Many of these sons and daughters would never return home. Christian churches were filled with millions who had the faith to believe that God was in control and that everything was going to be alright.

Today's generation lives in houses with two and three automobile garages; belongs to country clubs; eats in fine restaurants; sends their children to private schools and universities; has exotic vacations, and for many, a condo at the beach or in the mountains.

There is money or plastic to spend on multiple tastes today which were not available in previous years. God has truly blessed America.

There aren't enough hours in the day to meet the desires and tastes of the masses. Church attendance and the worship of God have been placed on the back burners, not temporarily, but permanently by many. Revivals may come and go in America, but only to meet temporary needs or crisis.

✣ AMERICA: A CHRISTIAN NATION?

Many in the USA took issue when former president, Barack Obama, made the statement that America was no longer a Christian nation. What he said has been interpreted in several ways. He was correct if his intent was to say that Christianity had lost its zeal and had comprised its message to appease America's cultural society and the age of political correctness.

It's often said that we are only one generation removed from total paganism. Many of today's parents are too busy to teach the Bible or values at home to their children. Many mothers and fathers have relegated their responsibilities to schools and churches.

Moses had these words from Yahweh about our responsibilities:

> Teach them to your children, talking about them when you sit at home and when you walk along the road, when you lie down and when you get up. Write them on the doorframes of your houses and on your gates. (Deut. 11: 19-20).

Recently on the evening news, there was a story about a family who had banned the latest technological devices and cellphones during meals. A mother realized there wasn't any communication happening with one another.

This is true in many places, not only in America, but throughout the world. Daily, people are losing their lives by walking into moving traffic: their eyes on the latest technological gadget. On sidewalks and streets, others are ignored. While driving and texting, we endanger not only ourselves, but those around us.

Americans are moving away from communicating personally with one another. Husbands and wives, parents and children, friends and neighbors might eventually wish that they had taken more time in communicating with those around them.

CHAPTER THREE

MOVEMENTS AND THEIR IMPACT

+ ## CAUSES, REASONS AND TRENDS WHICH ARE HAVING AN IMPACT ON THE KILLING OF THE CHRISTIAN CHURCH IN AMERICA

* CHURCH CLOSINGS
* DECLINING MEMBERSHIP
* FEWER BAPTISMS
* INFILTRATION BY NON-BELIEVERS
* STRIFE WITHIN DENOMINATIONAL CHURCHES
* SEXUAL ABUSE AND CORRUPTION WITHIN THE CHURCH
* LGBTQ MOVEMENT WITHIN CHURCHES
* RACISM
* LIBERAL TEACHING WITHIN LEARNING INSTITUTIONS
* GOSPEL MESSAGE NOT BEING PREACHED
* TELEVANGELISTS
* MEGACHURCHES PREACHING A PROSPERITY GOSPEL
* GAY AND ATHESISTS MINISTERS
* VOCATIONAL MINISTERS
* LIBERAL TEACHINGS WITHIN CHURCHES
* DEATHS OF THE ELDERLY
* CULTS AND WORLD RELIGIONS
* MILLENNIALS AND ACTIVISM MOVEMENTS
* CULTURAL LEANINGS
* CONSTITUTIONAL INTERPRETATIONS
* IGNORANCE OF GOD'S WORD
* TELEVISION AND MEDIA

* CHURCH GOERS BEHAVING LIKE THE LOST
* THE FAILURE OF CHURCHES TO FULFIL ITS
  PURPOSE
* THE COMING WRATH OF GOD

THE ABOVE LISTED MOVEMENTS PLAY A PART IN THE
imminent killing of the Christian church in the United States.
I will elaborate on some of these by giving more emphasis
to some rather than to others. Regardless of emphasis,
each of these causes, reasons and trends play a part in
***THE KILLING OF THE CHRISTIAN CHURCH IN
AMERICA.***"

God is not through with his invisible church. It will exist
until Jesus' return to claim those who have repented and put
their faith in Him. God, however, has already exited from
many churches who still proclaim His name. A minority of
Christians will remain in these structures until their closing.

The Holy Spirit will continue to live inside those who
have been born again. There will always be Christians among
the population of billions. Their Christianity will be like the
catacombs during ancient times, hidden from public view.

God is always in control. The people inside these wood,
brick and mortar buildings who are claiming a son and
daughter relationship with God need to be about the business
of the Lord.

Great and mighty is the One who holds us in His hands.
He offers this invitation to everyone:

> If my people, who are called by my name, will
> humble themselves and pray and seek my face and
> turn from their wicked ways, then I will hear from
> heaven, and I will forgive their sin and will heal
> their land" (2 Chron. 7:14).

Some attribute the saying *"It ain't over till the fat lady sings"*
to Yogi Berra, a former New York Yankee baseball player,

coach and manager. Some make claims that the phrase was first used by Dan Cook, a sportscaster, in April 1978, when he mentioned that the *"opera wasn't over till the fat lady sings."* Other claims are made as to when this saying was first used. Regardless of the origination of this saying, God, in His timeframe, will be the one who will bring everything to an end.

Church folks have stood for years in pews singing *"When We All Get to Heaven,"* a hymn written by Eliza Edmunds Hewitt in 1898. The hymn is seldom sung today in Christian churches. The multitudes of those who stood to sing this great old hymn have been given a new song to sing in heaven. These believers have reached their destination.

CHAPTER FOUR

WAYS TO EVALUATE YOUR CHURCH

STEPHEN GRAY AND FRANKLIN DUMOND IN THEIR book, *"Legacy Churches,"* written in 2009, list Six Indicators of Potential Closure:

> *"1. Public Worship Attendance Has Drastically Declined.*
>
> *2. Staffing of Essential Ministries Is No Longer Adequate or Effective.*
>
> *3. Annual Income is No Longer Adequate to Do Effective Local Ministry.*
>
> *4. The Church Has Not Consistently Grown Over the Last Five Years.*
>
> *5. The Age or Tenure of the Membership Is Unusually High.*
>
> *6. Survival Has Become the Main Mission."*

Their book gives detailed information on ways to evaluate a church in its present-day circumstances. These writers give some vital information in making an evaluation of present-day circumstances within a church.

✣ TAKE AN INVENTORY

Here's a questionnaire which I have developed for a church member to use.

You may know whether the church which you are attending is dead or alive by considering and responding to some of the following questions:

How many baptisms has your church had in the past few years? Were they adults or only the children of parents who are members of the church?

Are your baptisms keeping pace with the population growth in the community, town or city where your church is ministering?

Is the church which you are attending increasing or declining in membership or only keeping pace by transfers from other churches and denominations? Are these transfers keeping pace with your transfers and deaths?

Is the elderly makeup of the congregation in excess of fifty percent or more?

Is it primarily the elderly supporting the church through tithes and offering?

Has your church benefitted through large bequests from deaths and are these extra funds paying some bills or supporting the upkeep of the church?

Is your church reaching people in the community?

Is it reaching people from other races or nationalities?

Is English the only language spoken by people in the church?

Does your church have a young persons' Bible study class for ages eighteen through twenty-eight years of age? For young married and for singles?

Is your church willing to offer space to other Christian groups such as Hispanics or other foreigners?

Does your church offer only one preaching service which is a traditional service provided at 10:30 or 11:00 on Sundays?

Is there a ministry within your church which addresses the needs of college aged people and young married couples?

With exception of the Bible study meetings on Sunday before the morning service, are various Bible study meetings held during the week?

During the Bible study on Sunday morning, is the Bible being taught, or are books, current events and the opinions of others being discussed?

Do you have to entice members to attend a mid-week prayer service by offering a meal?

Do you provide a meal or other refreshments to get attendance at other functions during the week?

Is your church interested more in curtailing activities during the summer months or to continue with their regular activities?

Is your church canceling some of their regular meetings in order to participate in the viewing of football games such as the Super Bowl? Or if Halloween falls on a Wednesday when a prayer meeting is scheduled, which one takes precedence?

Are your deacons or elders doing the tasks which they were biblically called to do or basically doing nothing but offering leadership advice?

In your opinion, is your priest, minister, pastor or reverend, a true man of God? Has he been called by God or is it only a vocation?

Do church members prefer mission trips or tours to third world countries instead of making visits to the unchurched in their neighborhood?

Is the ministry of entertainment and socializing more important within your church than its ministry to a fallen world?

What is the youth of your church led to believe about ministry? Would they come without the benefits of being entertained?

How many young people do you have in your church?

Will the middle-aged membership be large enough to replace the elderly?

These listed questions are meant to survey your present situation in order to look at the future and to see how close your church might be to closing its doors.

✢ A PERSON'S MOTIVATION

I have been involved in jail and prison ministries for decades. The inmates who attend a period of fourteen weeks for Bible study classes often get accused by other inmates of *"coming for the chicken,"* at the conclusion of the study.

Imagine a felon, whether saved or unsaved, sitting through a long course of Bible study just to get a few pieces of fried chicken at the close of the study. If not a Christian, the felon would have to be addicted to fried chicken to endure twenty-eight hours of Bible study.

What motivates a person to attend church functions whether in prison or on the outside? This could be the same question for youth. What are their motivations? Do they attend for the entertainment, because they are forced to participate by parent, or their own free will?

Whatever the motivation, God says in his Word,

> "So is my word that goes out from my mouth: it will not return to me empty, but will accomplish what I desire and achieve the purpose for which I sent it" (Isa. 55: 11).

God's Word should be read at any church meeting and any church related activity.

✢ A DIFFERENT DAY AND TIME

Churches are closing their doors because God's blessings are no longer present. The purpose and mission of the church have been forgotten. Throughout the centuries, churches have remained open despite the absence of God's Spirit. The absence or exit of God's Spirit from churches hasn't been realized or missed by the membership. God's Spirit has been gone for years from some churches without its being realized by the membership.

The above stated observations are by no means meant to be critical or negative of a church. This writing isn't a vendetta. Questions are purposely stated for members of today's churches to evaluate whether their church is on a narrow path leading to life or on a wide road leading to destruction.

Today's culture is completely different from the culture of the 1950s and 1960s. In less than seventy-five years, Christianity has lost it power and appeal among the masses. The culture changes from one generation to the next, but the Holy Bible hasn't.

Within many denominational churches, the gospel is not being preached and young people are not being reached. This is also a reason why churches are being closed every day. Some pastoral staffs have given up on trying to reach people and have turned away from an evangelical message and are devoting their efforts to social activities. You will find more and more churches offering more meals and social activities to attract attendance.

The age of knocking on doors is obsolete and antiquated. Church members are no longer welcomed, and neither are solicitors of any type. The day of dropping-in unannounced has gone by the wayside.

Thanks be to the Lord God that some people will still seek spiritual nourishment. There are millions upon millions of people who are seeking answers to their problems whether physical, mental, emotional, spiritual or a hunger for truth. Some Sunday visits to churches will continue by those who are seeking answers to emptiness and purpose for their lives. And, there will be visits by those who are looking for the perfect church.

Every Sunday in churches throughout America, people will continue to visit who are hungry for something new which will bring happiness, peace and joy. For many of these visitors, the one and a half-hour on Sundays becomes only a pause that mildly refreshes. Some visitors will search for answers to their lostness and loneliness. Few decisions will be made to accept a church's invitation to join.

The most prosperous larger churches will continue to televise their worship service which will reach into the homes of millions. Those who choose to listen at home will see, hear, decide or reject and move from channel to channel seeking some satisfaction for their emptiness. Very few of these television viewers will ever visit a church. Some hearers will never open a Bible, believing or rejecting anything which comes out of the minister's mouth.

How are people to be reached by churches in this day and time? It will be through the way Christians live their lives after walking out the doors of a worship service on Sunday. It will be in schools, workplaces, restaurants, malls, shopping centers, supermarkets, sporting events, gym, and out on the streets. Today's masses prefer seeing a sermon than hearing one.

The lifestyle of a Christian is to be different from those who are without Christ. The eyes of the world are on the actions and lifestyles of those who make claims to their relationship with Christ.

CHAPTER FIVE

THE OLD TESTAMENT

✢ THE OLD TESTAMENT ERA

GOD'S PLAN AND PURPOSE FOR HUMANITY IS REVEALED in the Old Testament. Through many prophecies in the Old Testament, God sent His one and only unique son into the world to live among us, be crucified, and die for our sins. Jesus would not only die, but also be raised from death.

The Old Testament tells of God's perfect plan for his creation. Adam and Eve foiled God's plan by being disobedient. Due to the fall of man, forgiveness for our sins and a reconciliation to God became impossible, until an atonement could be made.

Some believers ask today if the Old Testament is relevant and should it still be a part of the Holy Bible. The Old Testament is the foundation for the Christian faith. Both the Old Testament and the New Testament mesh today into one book.

God, throughout the Old Testament period, raised up prophets who, by their preaching, would call His chosen people to repent and to return to obedience. These prophets were not only abused but were killed by religious leaders, and by those who refused to listen.

The prophet, Jeremiah, is a good example of a God-called preacher. Before he was born, God called Jeremiah to be his spokesperson to the people. The Lord God reached out his hand and touched his lips, saying,

"I have put my words in your mouth. See, today I appoint you over nations and kingdoms to uproot and tear down, to destroy and overthrow, to build and to plant" (Jer. 1: 9-10).

(There was a great deal of turmoil during Jeremiah's lifetime. For one thing, the temple was destroyed, and the Babylonian captivity began.)

This is what God-called preachers are to do today: to speak God's words and not their own words. Preachers are not sent by God to please their parishioners. God has already had plenty of false prophets telling folks that there is peace when there is no peace.

Listeners should evaluate the messages being preached from today's pulpits. Are these God's words or only words to appease those who are being catered to by the one delivering the message? Today pulpiteers are aware of those in their congregations who are the influential ones or the ones who are ravishing them with attention and praises.

Jeremiah was not called to please the people because God had put the words in the prophet's mouth which were to be spoken. God's message was one of repentance on the part of the people and a call not to choose other gods. The Israelites wanted none of that. They were satisfied with their way of life. Things were going well for them without having to worship the true God. That is the mindset of today's masses.

The Israelites dealt more harshly with Jeremiah than the way ministers are treated today. They wanted to kill him. Ministers in some denominations, when winning disfavor with their parishioners, are dealt with.

In addition to the prophets, the Lord God sent judges, priests, and kings to warn the people to repent and return to Him. But the Israelites wanted their own way and their own gods.

God is a forgiving and gracious Creator. He is the One who gives second chances to those who stumble, fall and depart to their own ways. He is patience and long suffering and warns His people of the consequences of their disobedience. These warnings often fall on empty ears. In America today, the masses believe that their ways have brought them to prosperity and well-being. God isn't necessary when we are doing so well on our own.

God knew before the beginning of time that mankind would go his own way. He made a final effort by sending His Son, Jesus Christ and His Holy Spirt into the world. God gives a free will to everyone to choose his way or to refuse.

God has been removed from the schools, public lands, courthouses, higher learning institutions and social, city and federal meetings throughout America. Because the removal of God, his presence and blessings will no longer be extended to churches and this nation.

God has given humanity many examples and warnings.

CHAPTER SIX

CHRISTIANITY'S BEGINNING

✣ THE NEW TESTAMENT ERA

THE BOOKS OF THE NEW TESTAMENT ANNOUNCED THE birth and teachings of the Messiah, Jesus Christ, God's only unique Son. He was rejected by the religious parties, crucified, and buried in a rich man's tomb. Repentance, as John the Baptist and Jesus preached, was rejected by the masses.

The Israelites of that day knew the Old Testament Scriptures to some degree but failed to properly understand what their expected Messiah would be. If he were to be the son of a former king by the name of David, he had to be a warrior who would set the people free from the Roman Empire. Jesus, riding into Jerusalem on a donkey a week before his crucifixion, was not representative of a dashing anachronistic on the back of a white stallion.

The religious parties of that day watched Jesus' every move. Even before Jesus physically tried to clean the corruption from the temple, the Sanhedrin knew that it was time for Jesus to go.

The Israelites didn't want anything to upset their way-of-life. Change to a person's lifestyle are not always easily accepted. Change affect everyone. Changes are out of the question.

The Jewish people and their leaders didn't want anything to upset their Roman overlords, fearing that a riot would cause harsher punishment for them. Jesus was taken by the religious leaders before Pilate, the Roman governor. Only the Romans could put a person to death. The Jews were successful in their quest to have Jesus put to death. The Roman way was to be the only way. Only Jesus' death on a cross would appease his accusers.

From its beginning, the first Christian church was begun in Jerusalem on the day of Pentecost. It probably included all types of people from varying occupations: fishermen, tax collectors, bookkeepers, farmers, shepherds, the poor, the wealthy, homeowners, landowners, housewives, and some widows. All of them were sinners who had been saved by their personal faith in Christ, and who believed that Jesus had been raised from the dead by the power of God.

The first Christian church was a small group: numbering one hundred-twenty or more members. This number rapidly increased on the day of Pentecost by the addition of three thousand more believers. Jesus' crucifixion on a cruel Roman cross was not the end of Christianity, but the beginning.

These saved sinners met in differing home settings: praying, rejoicing, eating, and having everything in common. There was no sacrifice too great for some who sold homes and land and gave their monies or a tithe to the church.

The established Jewish religious parties: the Sadducees, Pharisees and the Herodians, (who were more a political party,) took issue with this new religious movement. Dire methods were rapidly taken by them to stamp out its spread. The teachings of Jesus did not mesh with the teachings of these parties or the message which they had been presenting to their followers. It ran contrary to their beliefs.

Christianity, in its earlier stages, was not recognized by the Roman Empire as a religion. In its beginning, it was recognized by officials of the Roman Empire as a cult. Some referred to it as *"The Way."* During the reign of the Emperor, Constantine the Great, AD 306-357, Christianity began its transition to becoming the dominant religion of the Roman Empire.

Jesus, while walking the earth, had been confronted time after time by these mentioned parties, the Sadducees and the Pharisees were more dominant in their opposition to his message. The Herodians joined forces with the Pharisees to confront Jesus on one occasion in the Bible:

> Then the Pharisees went out and laid plans to trap him in his words. They sent their disciples to him along with the Herodians. "Teacher," they said, we know that you are a man of integrity and that you teach the way of God in accordance with the truth. You aren't swayed by others, because you pay no attention to who they are. Tell us then, what is your opinion? Is it right to pay the imperial tax to Caesar or not?" (Matt. 22: 15-17)

There were differences among these groups. The Sadducees didn't believe in an afterlife. The Pharisees did. The Herodians leaned more to the politics of Herod the Great.

The Sadducees and Pharisees were members of the Sanhedrin, a body of seventy-one members plus the high priest. The Sadducees were keepers of the temple, and the Pharisees and scribes were protectors of the law. The Roman government worked with the Sanhedrin, (their authority rested only in Judea) in keeping the peace. This Jewish body was abolished after the destruction of the Temple in Jerusalem around AD 70.

After the crucifixion of Jesus, his apostles were instructed by the Sanhedrin to NOT speak the name of *'Jesus.'* Though threatened and bodily beaten, the apostles would not keep quiet.

> Then they called them in again and commanded them not to speak or teach at all in the name of Jesus. But Peter and John replied, "Which is right in God's eyes: to listen to you, or to him? You be

the judges! As for us, we cannot help speaking about what we have seen and heard" (Acts 4: 18-20).

Stephen, a lay worker in the church at Jerusalem, is the first Christian martyr. His preaching about Jesus, which is mentioned in Acts, led to his death. It is believed by some scholars and students of the Bible, that all apostles were martyred with one exception, John, the apostle, who wrote five of the New Testament books, The Gospel according to Saint John, the three epistles of John and the book of Revelation.

✤ A MIGHTY MAN OF GOD

Saul, a Pharisee, was sent by the Sanhedrin to wreak havoc on this fast-growing Christian movement. Letters from the Sanhedrin gave Saul the authority to arrest the disciples of Jesus and to bring them to trial.

Saul, as Paul was also known, on the road leading to Damascus had a personal meeting with Jesus. The old Saul died, and the new Paul was made alive. He now exclaimed,

> I have been crucified with Christ and I no longer live, but Christ lives in me. The life I now live in the body, I live by faith in the Son of God, who loved me and gave himself for me (Gal. 2:20).

Many Christians believe that God changed the name of Saul to Paul. Saul was a Hebrew name and Paul was a Greek name. In Acts, chapter 13, Paul is still being referred to as Saul. There were others in the Bible who had two names or more. An example would be the apostle Peter. God did do changes in Paul's life, but didn't change his name.

Jesus appointed Paul an apostle and gave him direction. Paul, through the power of the Holy Spirit, wrote various Christian doctrines which are used by today's churches.

Dr. Luke, the writer of the Book of Acts or the Act of the Apostles began his writing of Acts by highlighting the ministry of the Apostle Peter. Soon after the conversion of Paul, Dr. Luke highlighted the preaching and missionary work of Paul and seldom made mention of Peter in later chapters.

✢ THE PURPOSE OF THE CHURCH

After the death and resurrection of the Lord, Jesus gave a command to his believers and to every Christian today:

> "Therefore go and make disciples of all nations, baptizing them in the name of the Father and of the Son and the Holy Spirit, and teaching them to obey everything I have commanded you" (Matt. 28: 19-20a).

There shouldn't be any doubt by denominations as to what is the mission and purpose of Christian churches. It is to evangelize the world for Christ. When a Christian church departs from that stated purpose, it's no longer doing the work of the Lord God.

Out in the consumer world, businesses try to improve their products. There is always something new. Coca Cola and other beverage makers desperately try to come up with new tastes. So do other companies.

If you are asked to pick up a certain brand of cereal, a person will need to know whether you want a banana, strawberry flavored cereal or other flavors. The same is true with toothpaste and numerous other items.

✢ TODAY'S CHURCHES HAVE MANY MENUS

Churches are guilty of doing similar things. Programs after programs are added or changed to entice parents to visit and become part of the membership. Some of these programs don't include the gospel message and becomes only an effort to increase church rolls and add financial support to an already failing ministry.

The social aspect is being emphasized more and more within the walls of a church and less and less is heard about the gospel of Christ. Entertainment, meals, social gathering and activities have become the norms.

The Apostle Paul exclaimed to the Church at Corinth this message:

> Now, brothers and sisters, I want to remind you of the gospel I preached to you, which you received and on which you have taken your stand. By this gospel you are saved, if you hold firmly to the word I preached to you. Otherwise, you have believed in vain. For what I received I passed on to you as of first importance: that Christ died for our sins according to the Scriptures, that he was buried, that he was raised on the third day according to the Scriptures, and that he appeared to Cephas and then to the Twelve (1 Cor. 15: 1-5).

This gospel message becomes the cornerstone of each church which claims the name of Jesus. When presenting Heaven to the masses, there isn't another way or name other than that of Jesus which offers a way of repentance and forgiveness for a person's sins.

God is being removed from public facilities due to the claims of some that it violates their constitutional rights. Christians have become ashamed to speak the name of God in their workplaces and outside the walls of a church. Christians don't want to offend others by exposing them to their beliefs. Christians are being told that this is the age of political correctness. No longer should we say *"Merry Christmas"* when we are in a holiday mood. *"Happy Holidays"* is now the norm.

The adaptation of cultural ways by the churchgoing public are fast approaching the complete rejection of the ways of biblical teachings. If the truth were known, some churchgoers are patterning their lifestyles to the ways of present-day culture.

Recently, it became national news when a minister mentioned that God appoints and places into authority those of His choosing. He had placed on his church's marquee a message which was considered political by his support of President Trump. Some in the neighborhood wanted the message on the marquee removed. The issue of the separation of church and state had been violated were the claims. The minister refused to comply with the threats of losing his present status as a tax-free institution. He was quoting from the Holy Word where it's written, "God does appoint and place in authority those of His choosing."

The Apostle Paul in his letter to the Romans wrote:

> Let everyone be subject to the governing authorities, for there is no authority except that which God has established. The authorities that exist have been established by God. Consequently, whoever rebels against the authority is rebelling against what God has instituted, and those who do so will bring judgment on themselves. For rulers hold no terror for those who do right, but for those who do wrong. Do you want to be free from fear of the one in authority? Then do what is right and you will be commended. For the one in authority is God's servant for your good. But if you do wrong, be afraid, for rulers do not bear the sword for no reason. They are God's

servants, agents of wrath to bring punishment on the wrongdoer (Romans 13: 1-4).

Of course, these Scriptures are questioned by those who find fault with those who are in positions of power. Their reasoning is that we aren't under the authority of those whom we believe to be ungodly rulers. God has allowed and permitted these ungodly leaders to attain their positions. It's only when rulers go against the teachings of God that we are to disobey their leadership.

If there is the separation of church and state, why do so many politicians who are running for a political office use the pulpits of churches to promote their political campaigns? And, why do churches permit this? It appears that only conservative Caucasian churches are targeted where there is criticism of separation of church and state. And another question: Why do politicians who have never been affiliated with a church, join a church when running for a political office?

Christians are to blame when they remain silent about what is happening each day to Christianity in America. By their silence, Christians have begun a journey to the catacombs of America. The early Christians, out of fear for their lives, went underground during the Roman era. Not yet in America do Christians fear for their lives. This is not true for some professing Christians in other places in the world.

It's not out of fear that we are going underground with our beliefs, but because our beliefs are offensive to others.

CHAPTER SEVEN

CENTURIES OF CHRISTIANITY

THE JEWS IN EARLIER TIMES DIDN'T WANT ANYTHING TO upset their way-of-life. Things have not changed for present day Christianity. The masses don't want anyone or anything to interrupt their way of living. Change is out of the question.

The Jewish people didn't want to upset their Roman captors by having Jesus around. A riot by Jews would cause harsher punishment from their Roman captors. Jesus had to be put to death since he was causing unrest among those who had been intimidated by his teachings. The Sanhedrin had no authority to put anyone to death. The Romans only had this authority.

The religious parties brought Jesus to Pontius Pilate, a Roman governor, because he had the authority to issue a death sentence. The religious leaders were successful in their quest to have Jesus put to death. The Roman way was to be the only way...death on a cross.

✣ THROUGH THE CENTURIES

From the Old and New Testament eras until the present age, the Lord God has called and sent numerous preachers and prophets in an-effort-to call his people to turn from their sinful ways of disobedience.

Some of the theologians and preachers sent to spread the gospel message after Peter and Paul are Polycarp (2nd century), Augustine and Jerome (5th century), Gregory the

Great (6th century), Thomas Aquinas (13th century), John Calvin, John Knox and Martin Luther (16th century), John Milton (17th century), Jonathon Edwards, John Wesley, George Whitefield (18th century), William Booth, Charles Finney, Charles Spurgeon, Billy Sunday (19th century), Karl Barth, C. S. Lewis, Reinhold and Richard Niebuhr, John Stott, Paul Tillich and A.W. Tozer (20th century), and John Piper (21st century). Listing these few names among so many other well-known theologians, isn't meant to imply that the author endorses or approves of all their interpretations of the Holy Bible.

Many brilliant and devout ones have been sent by God over the centuries to interpret and preach God's Word. Some of the more recent ones, which the reader or their grandparents may have heard them preach, are men who made an impact on this nation with their God-given talents of presenting His message.

Some will remember or have heard the likes of Charles Spurgeon (1834-1892, Dwight L. Moody (1837-1899), J. D. Grey (1906-1985), Herschel H. Hobbs (1907-1985), W. A. Criswell (1909-2002), and R. G. Lee (1909-2002). Dr. Lee preached his well-known sermon, *Payday Someday,* around the world some one thousand plus times.

I had the God-given opportunities to hear Dr. Criswell, J. D. Grey and R. G. Lee at churches where they pastored for many years. They were not only teachers of the Word, but God called preachers. I was privileged to hear Dr. Billy Graham at crusades in Los Angeles and Pensacola.

Some readers will remember the Brush Arbor days, which started in the late 1700's and existed into the mid-1900's. Circuit riding preachers went from town to town preaching the good news. These meetings were usually for one or two days and some went for a week or more.

Then, there were the *"tent"* days when revivals were conducted by traveling evangelists from town to town and county to county. These tent revivals stayed for several days until the people dwindled. These were the days when people had little money to spend and television and sporting events were not a ready distraction.

From the 1950s until churches stopped having revival meetings, there were evangelists booking revivals with congregations who had the funds to pay for their services. Many of these evangelists were flashy, wearing red ties and carrying red Bibles. Their wrist, shoes and socks all had the same color. It was more flash than class.

✣ AN INFLUENCIAL EVANGELIST

In 1947, America began to experience Dr. Billy Graham, who began his ministry eventually reaching millions not only in America, but also throughout the world. His message was a simple gospel message which tugged at the heart of listeners who were hungry for something which the world couldn't provide.

Dr. Graham was an unusual man. (He was called by God to present Jesus to the world.) And aren't we all? Christian churches all over the USA, filled buses loaded with members to participate in his revivals. He was not like the so-called television evangelists who lived in mansions and had lavish lifestyles. He received a salary from his evangelistic organization. Presidents and politicians relished his council and sought Dr. Graham's endorsements. It is my belief that he never did endorse anyone.

✣ THE IMPACT OF MOVIES AND TELEVISION

Before Dr. Graham began his crusades, *Gone with The Wind*, (1939) was released at a premiere in Atlanta, GA. When Rhett Butler made the comment, *"Frankly my Dear, I don't give a damn,"* millions of people within the United States were appalled. This was unthinkable language for the motion picture screen.

Then, just a few years later, along came *The Outlaw*, with Jane Russell. The motion picture industry was getting bolder and bolder. In the present age, pornography is presented on the screen without any appalment. Christian parents are having to screen and block these openly displayed acts from their children. Yet, many of these same parents are fascinated by these movies and watch them behind closed doors.

In 1956, Elvis first appeared on the Ed Sullivan show. He had first appeared on the Steve Allen show, which, being in the same time slot as the Ed Sullivan show, had outdrawn the Sullivan's show almost two to one.

Mr. Sullivan was not sure that he wanted Elvis on his show, since Elvis' gyrations, Sullivan felt, might be too provocative and sensual for television. But, for Mr. Sullivan to compete for television audiences with a competitor, Elvis was invited and his below the waist movements were not shown.

In the Sixties, the Beatles and Rolling Stones made their mark on America. It was a time when the assassinations of President John F. Kennedy, Martin Luther King, Jr., and Attorney General Robert Kennedy occurred.

President Lyndon B. Johnson and his Great Society programs came into existence in the 1960's. Some white pastors were preparing sermons to deal with and to disagree with the integration of their churches by black activists.

America was becoming wide open for any activity which gradually step-by-step was beginning to take a foothold. Churchgoing folks were too busy to take notice of movements which were gradually beginning to take shape in America. People catered to the money-making schemes from the broadcasting networks and the ways of Hollywood. Movie actors were becoming celebrities and role models to the younger population.

Church members were becoming wealthier. One car ownership became two. One home became another home at the beach or in the mountains. Instead of attending church on Sundays, outside interests, recreational activities, and even golf and fishing drew church members away from regular attendance and participation in the church. As the years passed, three preaching services a week would soon become one sermon per week in many churches.

Television not only took over the airwaves but captured the hearts of America and the entire world. Networks became bolder and bolder with the spreading of pornography and profanity. What would have caused a washing of our mouths with soap and water by our parents had become an acceptable practice by the viewing public. Suggestive contents on the networks were no longer left to one's imagination. A person could now see the real thing.

Today, some participants in game shows, when being introduced by the game show host, will acknowledge their Christianity. But later in their quest for answers to the questions being asked, dispel their Christianity by giving answers which once were only discussed behind closed doors at home.

CHAPTER EIGHT

DEFINING BELIEVERS AND UNBELIEVERS

✢ TODAY'S CHURCH ROLLS ARE FULL OF UNBELIEVERS

IN THIS BOOK, THERE WILL BE MUCH SAID ABOUT believers and unbelievers. It is necessary for readers to understand and distinguish between my use of these two words.

The use of the word *believer* as used in this book is a person who has a personal relationship with the Lord Jesus Christ. These individuals recognize their sinfulness and the need to repent and be forgiven by God for the wrongness which they have done. They realize that it isn't to mom and dad which they have been unfaithful, but to the God who created them: a God who is sinless and perfect in every way.

A sinful person cannot be made clean without the blood of Jesus washing away his or her uncleanness. Jesus answered,

> "I am the way and the truth and the life. No one
> comes to the Father except through me (John 14:6).

Many Bible-toting people will tell you how to be saved or become a *believer* but will say there are other additions such as baptism and good deeds which a person must do. Of course, a *believer* will want to be baptized and do good deeds after their salvation. However, baptism and doing good deeds will not bring forgiveness for our sins.

What Jesus did on the Cross when he died for our sins is sufficient:

> "I have been crucified with Christ and I no longer live, but Christ lives in me. The life I now live in the body, I live by faith in the Son of God, who loved me and gave himself for me." (Gal. 2:20).

> Therefore, if anyone is in Christ, the new creation has come: The old has gone, the new is here! (2 Cor. 5:17).

Salvation for a *believer* comes through faith:

> For it is by grace you have been saved, through faith - and this is not from yourselves, it is the gift of God - not by works, so that no one can boast" (Eph. 2: 8-9).

Much more could be said about a *believer*. But for now, who is an *unbeliever?*

An *unbeliever*, as defined in this book, is a person who is lost or unsaved, not having had a personal relationship with the Lord Jesus Christ, but whose name is on a church's membership role. He or she doesn't have to be an atheist or an agnostic to be an *unbeliever.*

These are the ones who do not accept and do not have a personal relationship or born-again relationship with Jesus Christ. They may have infiltrated Christian churches, professed to the church that they hold to the church's beliefs, but are unrepentant and do not exercise their faith in the One who died for their sins. The sad part is that multitudes of *unbelievers* don't realize their lostness. The church is an institution where unbelievers come to find peace and fellowship. It is to them no more than a social club, a book club, a country club or dinner club.

An *unbeliever* may be sitting beside another *unbeliever* in the pews while throughout the congregation others are rubbing elbows with *believers* To the *unbeliever* the pastor is the president, the leader of the pack, but not a spiritual leader because *unbelievers* are unable to discern things pertaining to the Spirit. Some will tithe their earnings while others will give very little. They come, participate, relax and enjoy the one or more hours of what they have been taught or heard from their pastors, teachers, parents or by others. But are not saved.

✢ MEMBERSHIP LENIENCY

Churches are very lenient with their membership rules. In many churches, persons who come and ask for membership are never questioned about their faith while other churches may require new members to participate in *orientation classes.* Many of these classes will dwell on the functions, by-laws, opportunities and committees within the church, but not on a person's relationship with the Lord God. A church will take the word or statement of a potential member about their personal relationship with Christ because there isn't another way to know what is in the person's heart.

The requirements for membership in a church are different than those in clubs and organizations. One example is the American Legion. A person who completes an application for membership is required to show proof of having served in the Armed Forces. In some instances, persons have sought membership by claiming that they are veterans. These claimants are soon detected when their applications have been checked.

The same kind or type of thing applies when applying for employment with a company or corporation. Resumes are submitted and are checked for facts. Country clubs, organizations, colleges and universities have their own requirements for admission.

The *unbeliever* in many instances, is not being deceptive because he or she doesn't know and understand what the word *Christian* means. The only requirement in many Christian churches or denominations is that the person coming for membership professes to be a *believer*.

The word *Christian* is used three times in the New Testament and is not defined. It is interpreted by some Bible scholars to mean a person belonging to Christ and who is a follower.

CHAPTER NINE

NOTICEABLES AND UNNOTICEABLES

✣ THE DESIRE FOR NOTICEABILITY IS BECOMING MORE EVIDENT

IN WRITING ABOUT THE NOTICEABLE AND unnoticeable in this chapter, these two adjectives will be used as nouns, which is correct in some cases.

On every church roll in the USA, there are the NOTICEABLES and the UNNOTICEABLES.

The quest for recognition and authority by many church members has become more dominant in churches throughout America. Soon they become the most NOTICEABLES. Many of these noticeable ones will attain key positions. Many on church rolls have a desire for position, power and recognition within the church's body. This quest has never been satisfied in the secular world.

Noticeables are those members in a church who have assumed places of leadership and are the prevailing strong voices behind the many decisions which are made in both denominational and autonomous churches.

Noticeables are those who want to be recognized as key persons and to become the more important ones. Their desire is to dominate and have their way in many decisions which are made. Their pursuit of goals is made and carried out covertly, but also overtly.

✤ NOTICEABLES: BOTH UNBELIEVERS AND BELIEVERS

Once, when I was pastoring a church in Florida, a young man came asking what he could do within the church body. He wanted to know if there was something that needed to be done in and around the church. He was not asking for any renumeration, but if there was something which needed to be done which his talents would permit.

He was told that some members come each week, sweep the floors, vacuumed the carpets, wiped the pews, cut the grass and did some landscaping. "No!" he said. "You don't understand. I want my voice to be heard." It was then suggested that he meet with the choir director.

The young man joined the choir, and in a very few weeks, he stood before the congregation to sing a solo, even though it was evident he had not been given a musical talent by the Lord God. Later, not being satisfied by his present status, he volunteered to drive our young boys from a summer youth camp. On the way home with the youth, he stopped by a farmer's patch of watermelons to steal a watermelon for the young boys to eat. This young man was in search of recognition, not only on a Sunday, but sought acceptance from the youth as well. He was seeking a role of noticeability.

May forgiveness be given me by the Lord God should it not be permissible for me to question the faith of the person sitting beside me in the pew or the people who shakes my hand or those hugged before and after the service, as to their being true believers.

Noticeables are those who want to be seen, to be heard and to lead, those who in some instances appear dedicated individuals doing the work of the Lord. They work in the open inside and outside the doors of the church. Some show up during the week requesting an audience with the pastor, while some work behind the scenes at home by phone or other methods to keep their special agenda alive.

Some of these noticeables are those who have never repented of their sins and have never tasted the blood of our Lord and Savior. Primarily they are there for the recognition. They have failed to achieve the recognition which is their basic wish or desire.

It is true that all noticeables are not those who are unsaved. Some noticeables publicly appear before the church to fulfil God given tasks. These are not there for the recognition. God has given to them a calling and the necessary talents to do his work. They are the true children who love the Lord's work and the leadership of the Holy Spirit. They are the humble ones who are seeking only to satisfy their Lord.

Parents with children know about the desire, "Mother, Daddy, look at me or watch me!" Those words are familiar ones. When we didn't give our children our full attention, the cry for recognition grew louder and never abated until we adhered to their wishes.

There will always remain a burning desire in the hearts of some church members to be recognized by their peers. Undoubtedly, they didn't receive it at home by their mothers and fathers or their husbands or wives. This desire for recognition is prevalent in all of us, but in the lives of some, it's the overwhelming desire to be recognized.

✢ AN EXAMPLE OF A NOTICEABLES

While pastoring a church in the Northwest, one of the more dominant male members courted my attention. He was a very prominent member of the congregation and perhaps the wealthiest. When the church was split down the middle, he was the leader of one of the groups. He invited my family on several occasions to come to his home for dinner and to go fishing on his boat in Puget Sound.

On one occasion, he asked if I would like to meet the Campus Crusade for Christ founder, Dr. Bill Bright. What pastor in ministry for Christ Jesus would want to miss the opportunity of meeting the man who published the well-known booklet, *"Four Spiritual Laws?"* Together, the two of us traveled from Washington state to California to meet with Dr. Bright. What a blessing!

This wealthy member of the church finally confessed to me his desire to lead and to shape the direction of the church. He had gotten his way in the past, why not now? He admitted that the former pastor looked to him for leadership and often visited with him and his family at home. "It's not going to be that way with me," I said. I was now certain of his intentions by all the courtesies he has offered in the past.

When it became evident to him that he was going to be unable to lead me in his direction, he threatened to leave the membership and to take his tithe with him. "Do whatever the Lord leads you to do," I replied. He never left the church while I was pastor. He would become my thorn in the flesh.

Most noticeables are not as open with their desires and intentions as *"John"* was. They come forth as the devil and his angels do with overt and covert overtures. Desperation on the part of some to be seen and heard will lead to many tactics.

The sad part is that some noticeables don't realize that they are lost. Repentance and faith have never come to their forethoughts. These noticeables are under the impression, while satisfying their own needs, that the work which they are doing in the church will lead them by their efforts to the portals of Heaven.

I recently heard a message by a seminary theologian who included in his sermon, a conversation that he had with the late Dr. Billy Graham. "Dr. Graham, you said some years ago in some of your speeches that you believe fifty percent of the people who are members of churches are lost. Is that true?"

Dr. Graham responded by saying, "No. It's not true. I believe that it's more like seventy percent."

Whether this theologian, who was filling the pulpit at a Southern Baptist Church on a Sunday morning, was saying that Dr. Graham thought this was true of the SBC or all denominations, it wasn't made clear. It's my opinion that it's true of most SBC churches and most denominations in the United States.

I am trying not to be redundant, but I need to say it again: some of the noticeables who are in key positions in churches are Christians. Some hold leadership positions on various committees, truly serve as teachers, and become pillars of faith. These saved ones are in these key rolls because of their calling and the talents which God has given to them. They are not in it for the recognition afforded to noticeables who are unsaved and who will continue to seek attention.

✢ BUSINESS DEALINGS WITHIN THE CHURCH

Some noticeables are those who use the benefits of the church to sell their wares. Some pass out their business cards, making known the products which they offer. Some take orders while at church and make deliveries at church. This isn't to say that those using the church for business interests are not Christians.

Perhaps, I'm being harsh with those who are guilty of this practice. Our motive for attending church is to be none other than to worship the Lord and to learn of Him. Whether these noticeable(s) be donators, tithers or contributors to the budget of the church or give nothing at all, they receive free advertising for their wares.

I once attended a Methodist church where the pastor, when receiving new members into the church, gave a one-time opportunity to new members to state their occupations. More free advertising.

While attending a church where a major building project was going on, the mother of a son who had been given a key role in the project, made this statement about her son, who was also a member: "He will never in his lifetime have to worry about his financial security. This project will make him richer." Whether this man was a believer or unbeliever or a member only for financial gains, only the Lord knows.

When building projects occur at many churches, huge financial benefits are given to noticeables and unnoticeables in the church without any bids from outside businesses. Some of these members are the ones who travel from church-to-church looking for business opportunities. They get chummy with the leadership, make their presence known, and watch and wait for opportunities. It becomes a scratching-of-the back process and renumerations come to those making the decisions in the guise of a trip to the golf range, a week or weekend at a beach condo or even to a mountain cabin. The bigger the project, the greater the gift.

✢ DISTINGUISHING UNNOTICEABLES

As previously mentioned, some unnoticeables are Christians and some are not. Christian unnoticeables don't seek recognition. Most born again disciples understand the role of being a disciple of the Lord Jesus and some do not. Believers have been called by the Lord to make disciples of all nations beginning first at home. There isn't a viable way for one to distinguish unnoticeables who are true believers from the unsaved ones. Only God knows true believers.

In one parable which Jesus told, weeds were easy to distinguish from the good seeds which were sown:

> "But while everyone was sleeping, his enemy came
> and sowed weeds among the wheat, and went away.
> When the wheat sprouted and formed heads, then
> the weeds also appeared. The owner's servants
> came to him and said,' 'Sir, didn't you sow good
> seed in your field? Where then did the weeds
> come from?' "'An enemy did this,' he replied.
> "The servants asked him, 'Do you want us to go
> and pull them up?' "No,' he answered, 'because
> while you are pulling the weeds, you may uproot
> the wheat with them. Let both grow together until
> the harvest. At that time I will tell the harvesters:
> First collect the weeds and tie them in bundles to
> be burned; then gather the wheat and bring it into
> my barn'" (Matt. 13: 25-30).

The disciples, having heard Jesus' parable about the weeds, asked for an explanation of its meaning:

> He answered, "The one who sowed the good seed
> is the Son of Man. The field is the world, and the
> good seed stands for the people of the kingdom.
> The weeds are the people of the evil one, and the
> enemy who sows them is the devil. The harvest is
> the end of the age, and the harvesters are angels.
> As the weeds are pulled up and burned in the fire,
> so it will be at the end of the age. The Son of Man
> will send out his angels, and they will weed out
> of his kingdom everything that causes sin and all
> who do evil. They will throw them into the blazing
> furnace, where there will be weeping and gnashing
> of teeth. Then the righteous will shine like the sun
> in the kingdom of their Father. Whoever has ears,
> let them hear" (Matt. 13: 37-43).

To translate what is said by Jesus about weeds and wheat into modern day terminology within the membership of any church building there are good seed and evil seed. True believers are the wheat. The unsaved or lost ones are the weeds. Dr. Graham could be right in saying seven out of ten members in churches are lost, there is a tremendous weed population. Only the Son of Man and his angels can distinguish true believers from those who do not have a personal relationship with Him.

Some Christian unnoticeables and noticeables are the wheat who quietly go about the work of the Lord and who seek little or no recognition. These members love what they have been called to do over the years. Some of these reach elderhood status, and their former responsibilities are delegated to others. Believing that the younger generation is much more apt and capable than they, these elder ones shirk future responsibilities and begin to rest on their laurels. They now become members of those people who "use-to-do" certain functions in the church. That laurel is for some elderly, but not all.

Again, this isn't to say that all unnoticeables are true believers. By no means! As stated earlier, whether in the Southern Baptist Convention or in other denominations, unbelievers are in the majority.

Some unbelievers now dominate once very conservative churches which have now turned liberal in their theology. Saved members seeking more conservative teachings, leave and seek out churches with more conservative teachings. These more conservative churches are being found among the Church of God and Holiness groups as well as others. Some, saved and unsaved, who depart liberal churches don't look for another church. but return to the couch at home. Saved or unsaved, they remain unaffiliated.

✛ HOME SCHOOLING

Good mothers and fathers want the best for their children. Some families will not turn their children over to public schooling or to an academy. They do their own schooling. When it comes to Bible schooling at home, however, theology becomes an impossible task since so little about the Bible is known by parents.

Remember where the Scriptures were first taught after the Day of Pentecost? Believers met in their homes. Will it happen again? Parents are to be the teachers of their children. First century parents were absent of present-day venues.

Unbelieving noticeables and unnoticeables, without the church as a platform, will have to get noticed in other ways. The blind will have to find other ways to lead the blind.

CHAPTER TEN

RESEARCH: GATHER, SIFT, EVALUATE

✢ MANY CHURCH MEMBERS DON'T WANT TO GET INVOLVED IN THE CHURCH'S POLITICS

STUDENTS, ATTENDING INSTITUTIONS OF LEARNING, often participate in research projects to evaluate a situation. Students will gather information, sift some of the material, then do an evaluation by discarding some information and keeping some. After graduation, students entering vocations will do very little research except when an employer might require it.

This is primarily true of church members. Many will take for granted and not question many of the things which happens within the confines of the church. If something doesn't interfere with attendance, tithing or participation, why bother? After all, people are in church only a few hours each week, and many don't see a need to get involved. However, there are instances where change is made, and it could make a difference in one's beliefs.

While visiting with my daughter one Sunday in another state and at a church of a different denomination than mine, my wife and I attended her Bible study class. My daughter announced to the class that they would be moving to another classroom the next Sunday. The reason her class would be changing rooms was so the elderly could get closer to their classrooms from an entrance or an exit. This move would save the elderly time and distance from having to walk as far in entering and exiting the church.

She created a firestorm. Several calls were received that afternoon from some of the folks who would have to move. In fact, one head honcho in the church was very upset because the decision was made without his knowledge. This minor thing was very devastating to a few who didn't do any research or care about the reason. Changes in any situation are always upsetting. As members, we don't often take the time to ponder why certain changes are necessary.

When a church spends thousands of dollars on luncheons and meals or starts another program when a similar one is already in place, there should be questions. When the Bible is misquoted, misinterpreted, additions made, and said to be antiquated, questions should be raised and evaluated.

Members, perhaps due to timidity or not wanting to be targeted as negative, never question or let their voices be heard for such happenings. Taking issue with why this or that was done, members will subject themselves to being viewed as going against the grain.

Have you noticed when you're doing something around the house or even driving an automobile, how a large percentage of what you do is mechanical? Members go through mechanical motions in many activities while at church. Motions and changes are made without having a thorough understanding of the issues.

When members get involved in the politics of the church, they begin to see the big picture. And the big picture is not a pretty one. With this politics, you will come to the knowledge of why some members say *"my"* or *"our"* church instead of the Lord's church. One will soon begin to know who the noticeables and the unnoticeables are in the church. The quest for power and recognition and the intentions on the part of some, will become transparent.

Why do people go to a church which is being run to satisfy the desires of certain individuals?" Some reasons might surprise you when evaluating happenings which are not transparent. Researching of these reasons might be revealing. Many members depart from questioning and may decide that spirituality isn't necessary in certain functions of the church.

✧ REASON FOR ATTENDING CHURCH

The one true reason for attending church should be to worship the Lord and to learn of Him. There's nothing wrong with why a person goes to church if the reasons are *"it's the Lord's Day"* or *"to keep this day holy."* One can't worship the Lord unless you know Him and have had a personal relationship with his Son, Christ Jesus. Hearts should be challenged to research and evaluate why certain programs are necessary or unnecessary in carrying out worship and the Great Commission.

✧ AN EVALUATION OF YOUR CHURCH

For Christians, the ones who belong to Christ, there is always a need for self-evaluation and an evaluation of the happenings withing the church. This should lead to questions which search for answers to these questions.

There is the need for researching all functions of the church's programs to determine whether the church is fulfilling its mission. Some go to church, sit and listen, but never think. It's like walking or running on a treadmill. We climb on board, select the speed, change it often, get off after several minutes of running or walking. We dismount to find out that we haven't gone anywhere. It's the same as going to church. We come the same way we entered, and when we leave, we are still the same way spiritually.

One might ask: *"Is this what Christianity is about? Is this why the Lord Jesus died for our sins? Do I continue to worship in a church which appears to have lost its way? Should I let my voice be heard or remain silent and do nothing? If I move my membership to another church, will it be like the one that I am now leaving? Will I ever find the perfect church?"* The answer to the last question is an obvious "No." All churches are imperfect.

When Christians are members of a church for years and years, they become so friendly with the environment that they don't want to leave the church, which is being taken over by the unsaved. There will never be a starting over for some. The love for a wood, brick and mortar building, which has been home for so many years and full of so many memories of family and friends, will never be replaced.

✢ WHAT IS BEING SAID FROM PULPITS

Secondly, one of the major reasons to do research about the church or denomination which we have become a part of is to evaluate what is being said from the pulpit. The reading of the Bible in church doesn't mean that the Word of God is being preached or is being taught. An analytical mindset is needed. Some don't have analytical minds and questions are not raised as to what is said or preached whether it is biblical or unbiblical.

Before becoming a member of any congregation, some will attend several churches near their homes. They will get the *feel* of the church: it's warmth, the programs, the music, the makeup and the personality of the minister.

This ability to attend another church is mostly available to a more mobile society, but not for those grandparents and parents who have been members for decades. It is the expectation of parents, when their children arrive at the age of accountability, that they, too, become members of the same church.

Personally, that is why so many unsaved are on church rolls throughout America. Children and grandchildren, out of respect for parents and grandparents, make church a family affair. For many, there isn't any repentance, conversion or salvation in association with membership. Some of these will eventually come to a stage of repentance, having their personal relationship with the Lord Jesus and asking to be baptized again.

✢ WHAT IS BEING TAUGHT BY PASTORS AND TEACHERS

Thirdly, there should be a thorough analysis by church members of what pastors and teachers are delivering to their listeners. Are these teachings from pulpits and classrooms biblical or personal opinions?

Analyze the sermons and lessons which you are hearing. When sitting through a Bible study or a homily, try to research, in an objective way about what you have heard. Look for the spiritual aspects, if any.

In many modern-day churches, an outline of the sermon is displayed on a screen. Some of the three or four main topics of the sermon are partially left blank in their bulletins. Listeners often use their church's bulletin to scribble out what has been missing from the printed program. The intent of these scribbled notes is to do further study at home. In many cases, they will never be used again.

✢ THE EMPLOYMENT OF A SHEPHERD

Ministers are invited to stand before search committees to deliver trial sermons and have job interviews. Mainly, it's a one-sided affair. The potential prospect will go overboard in preparation, and the committee will evaluate the deliverer, trying to fit the applicant into the missing link of their chain.

In my younger day, more so than today, I was more passionate about foreign missionary work for the Lord. Today, I realize less the purpose or importance of doing ten days or a two-week journey to foreign shores when there is such a need to spread the Word of God in the community here at home. First century work by the apostles and disciples began at Jerusalem. The work of reaching the local community should be consistently before a church. Community first, foreign fields later.

Early in my ministry I was asked to preach a trial sermon for a search committee who would be coming from Lake Helen, FL. It was scheduled for a Sunday night away from their church. I preached on a text taken from the book of Jonah. This is a brief summary of what was preached:

> "God, because of his love for all of humanity, called Jonah to go to Nineveh and preach a message of repentance to its people. Jonah didn't want God to save a people who was not of his race. Jonah, due to his resistance and rebellion, ended up in the belly of a big fish which God had created. Jonah, after coming to his senses, and praying to God for deliverance, finally did what God had called him to do from the beginning."

After the sermon, one of the men on the committee shook my hand and said, *"Keep on preaching about those heathens in foreign lands."* Instantly I knew that there would be no further contact between me and the committee. The search committee knew within a twenty-five to thirty minutes span that I was not the missing link which they were looking for. They were looking for someone to reach their community.

✛ A Minister's Study Time

While attending the seminary, I was told by a professor that for each minute spent in the pulpit preaching, a pastor should spend one hour in Bible study. The professor was teaching that this was the right commitment for preparing a sermon. However, I believe it would be better spending the time on one's knees instead of searching through commentaries to find what scholars have written about the Scriptures.

In many denominations, folks bring their Bibles, I-pads, and other technological devices to services. With today's technology, they can instantly pull-up the Scriptures from which the minister is using and receive comments concerning what others have said about them.

Listen to every word spoken by the minister. Do your research at home. Allow God to speak to you during the service. Take what you can spiritually use and discard the rest. Search for the facts. Better still, let the Lord God speak to you from the pages of the Holy Bible.

CHAPTER ELEVEN

CULTS AND RELIGIOUS GROUPS

IN OUR PRESENT AGE OF SO MUCH TECHNOLOGY, IT IS appalling that there are so many cults and false religions which are thriving. Four to five thousand (or even more) cults and religious bodies throughout the world are spreading false doctrines. Manmade doctrines are taught, preached and practiced by millions in America.

Two well-known religious bodies, the Church of Jesus Christ of Latter-day Saints (Mormons), and Jehovah's Witnesses are recognized as pseudo Christian cults. Christian Science, Hinduism, Buddhism, and Scientology are cults. Bob Larson in his book *Larson's Book of Cults* list these and many other religious and recreational cults. A cult can be defined by its deviation from the Holy Word of God and its teachings. In Christian circles, "cult" is used for those claiming to be Christian but are not. World religions are thus not "cults."

A cult is defined as a religious group that denies one or more of the fundamentals of biblical truth. A cult holds views that are unorthodox and spurious. Cults are religious movements which make claims to being part of the Christian faith yet denies its truths.

✢ IDENTIFYING CULTS

Readers might question why in this book such time and effort is devoted to cults such as the Peoples Temple, the Church of Jesus Christ of Latter-day Saints and Jehovah's

Witnesses. These three recognizable religious bodies are among the numerous religious bodies which are defined as cults.

The importance for lengthiness in this writing is to consider the influence and impact which cults have in the lives of unbelievers and Christian churches worldwide. It's extremely difficult for those outside the teachings and understanding of God's Word to distinguish between truth and fiction. Cults do play a role in **THE KILLING OF THE CHRISTIAN CHURCH IN AMERICA.**

Cults in the USA and throughout the world are humanly made. The masses who are members of Bible teaching churches may ask, *"What difference does it make anyway? Let them do their thing and we will do ours."* Cults play a role leading the lost away from the God of the Holy Bible. Cults lead to the total confusion of those who are lost and to Christian church members as well.

Christianity is not a pick-and-choose religion. Neither is the Bible also. Those who choose to pick and choose from God's Word and who discard part of the Bible to please their own tastes and values seek to please themselves. Humans from these cults write their own Bibles while adding to and deleting what doesn't apply to their ideas.

When using a cafeteria type Bible menu for one's religious beliefs, there are many pitfalls. Cultists, believing that it's a road to a heavenly home, find themselves still in their sins and without cleansing. There is a tendency to choose what is most appealing when walking through a cafeteria line and deciding which food has the most appeal. Our taste buds dictate what we will choose. Choices can result with good food and bad food. A person's cultural lifestyle will choose what is most appealing when making spiritual choices.

Those who are in the workforce know that their employer, whether a small company or a large corporation, have rules and regulations which employees are expected to abide by. An employee doesn't have the prerogative to pick and choose what they like or dislike about an employer's requirements.

When it comes to various religions, however, some religious bodies offer to their parishioners a tasteful menu. Seeking a place of worship, the goal of any person should be in finding a Bible-teaching body where the true menu is God's Word without any modifications.

From the time of "in the beginning" to the present age, people have been led down many wide roads which have been chartered by men and women who have picked and chosen paths contrary to the teachings of God's Word. Hence, the startups of cults.

Someone will say: "I sincerely believe" or "others are sincere in their beliefs." Sincerity is not a path to heaven. The only path from our sinful nature is to be washed in the blood of the Lamb.

The Word of God in its entirety has survived throughout the ages. Manmade cults lead people down the wide roads which eventually will lead to destruction. Jesus had this to say about the roads which we travel each day:

> "Enter through the narrow gate. For wide is the gate and broad is the road that leads to destruction, and many enter through it. But small is the gate and narrow the road that leads to life, and only a few find it" (Matt. 7: 13-14).

The narrow road is difficult to find, while the broader one is more easily traveled.

The narrow road is more difficult to find while the wide one is more accessible. The narrow road leads to eternal life while the wide road leads to destruction and damnation. Cults lead people down the wide road which lead masses away from the truth of God's Word.

Webster's II New College Dictionary defines *"cult"* as 1. A community or system of religious worship and ritual. 2. (a) A religion or religious sect generally regarded as extremist or false, whose followers often live communally under an authoritarian, charismatic leader.

In the next three chapters three cults will be highlighted: one which is no longer in existence and two which appear to be thriving.

CHAPTER TWELVE

THE PEOPLES TEMPLE

A BRIEF LOOK AT A FORMER CULT WHICH LED TO THE deaths of hundreds:

James Warren Jones, Jr. (May 13, 1931 – Nov. 18, 1978) was born in Crete, Indiana. He was later known as the Reverend Jim Jones and led his followers into calling him "Father" or "Dad." Near the end of his life, he made claims to being Christ and even God.

Jim Jones, in 1956, founded the Peoples Temple, a racially integrated church in Indianapolis, IN. In its beginning, Jones' Peoples Temple was founded on helping the mentally ill, foster children, the elderly and addicts.

Receiving criticism from some circles, Jim Jones, with 65 families, moved his Peoples Temple from Indianapolis to Redwood Valley, CA, and eventually expanded his work into the San Francisco Bay area.

After making the move to California, the Peoples Temple became more political than religious and more communistic in it practice. The church transitioned into a church centered around its leader who was becoming more paranoid and unbalanced. With Jones gaining more and more power over his followers, public criticism and scrutiny began to grow about this movement. Jones became more paranoid by the criticism and claimed that the FBI, CIA and others in the federal government were out to get him.

Jones' top hierarchy pledged their devotion to their cult leader by pledging their material possessions and money. Some even signed over custody of their children to him.

Peoples Temple members believed Jones' promises of a better life in an environmental area under ideal conditions. Through violence and intimidation, Jim Jones and his hierarchy, maintained control of their followers.

In 1977, Jim Jones led his Peoples Temple from California to Jonestown, Guyana in South America. His followers were led to believe that conditions in this remote Guyana jungle were utopian and a perfect spot for their "Agricultural Project." Peoples Temple members believed Jones' promises of a better life in an environment area under ideal conditions. Through violence and intimidation, Jim Jones and his hierarch-maintained control of their followers.

In Guyana, Jones' power over his followers and his thirst for more authority became more horrible. Living conditions were becoming unbearable and the work hours longer for his followers.

In 1978, news of these atrocities in Guyana reached the office of Democratic U. S. congressman Joseph Ryan, Jr. who had been serving in capacity since 1973. He and a delegation flew to Guyana to investigate the claims being made by some of Ryan's constituents.

Among Ryan and his delegation, was a Ryan's staffer, Karen Lorraine Jacqueline Speier. Later, in 2008, she would begin to serve as the U.S. representative from California's 14th congressional district. Representative Speier was shot five times in what is now known as the Jonestown Massacre. Near her, Representative Leo J. Ryan and four others lay dead. Speier and nine others had been shot and left for dead at a remote airstrip in Guyana. They waited twenty-two hours for help to arrive.

Jim Jones, after these killings which happened on November 18, 1978, convinced his followers *that parachutes would be dropping from the skies and their babies killed*" and to drink poison labeled as "Kool Aid." Nine hundred eighteen (918) followers, including three hundred and four (304) children died.

Jim Jones died by a gunshot wound to his head. Some sources say the gun laid three feet from his body while others report it rested on his chest. Whether this gunshot to his head was self-inflicted or administered by another is not known. Some speculate that his personal nurse, Annie Moore, could have shot him and then took her own life by gunshot. It was reported that the gunshot that killed her did not come from the same weapon.

The story of Jim Jones and the Peoples Temple is a sad story to the world and especially to family members of the many lives lost to such a tragedy. His followers were misled by a power-hunger religious fanatic. These followers and their families were seeking a better life for themselves.

God made his final revelation to all nations when the Book of Revelation was written by the Apostle John:

> I warn everyone who hears the words of the prophecy of this scroll: If anyone adds anything to them, God will add to that person the plagues described in this scroll. And if anyone takes words away from this scroll of prophecy, God will take away from that person any share in the tree of life and in the Holy City, which are described in this scroll (Rev.22: 18-19).

Revelation was written as a distinct document and "this scroll" refers to Revelation alone, technically. However, my interpretation of this passage in Revelation is that God has nothing else to say or to reveal, and that nothing is to be changed or added to his Holy Book.

CHAPTER THIRTEEN

THE CHURCH OF JESUS CHRIST OF LATTER-DAY SAINTS (LDS)

✢ A LITTLE OVERVIEW

PRESENT DAY MORMONS EMBRACE MANY CHRISTIAN beliefs, yet have their own distinct doctrines, values and precepts. They are considered loving, kind and friendly people. Mormons follow a strict healthy lifestyle, and are not allowed alcohol, tobacco, coffee or tea. They believe in family values and have respect for authority.

Mormons are deceived by false teachings that distort the nature of God, the person of Jesus Christ and the means of salvation. They don't recognize the Trinity and believe that God, Jesus and the Holy Spirit are three separate Gods.

I have searched several websites including Wikipedia; MCH The Moroni Channel; exMormon.org; bible truths.net; rom.byu.edu; history.com; as well as Larson's Book of Cults to obtain much of the information which will be discussed here. Comments will also be made about my personal experiences with Mormons while living in Tacoma, WA.

✢ PERSONAL EXPERIENCES

As a pastor of a Southern Baptist Church in Tacoma, WA, I ministered in a community dominated by Latter-day Saints. I rang many doorbells at well-maintained, middleclass

Mormon homes in the area surrounding the Baptist church, but never was able to arouse anyone to open a door.

I don't believe that I was being ignored by the Mormon occupants. On the porches of many of these homes, there were packages from LDS businesses to the occupants which indicated that many were at work or were not home after UPS or Fed-X deliveries. Some of the packages which were seen on the porches of several homes probably contained *temple garments* which are worn by adult members in their ritual practices.

My purpose in visiting these homes was to introduce myself, get acquainted with those living in the community, and to offer an invitation to come visit the Baptist church within their neighborhood.

There were members of the church which I pastored who had family and friends who were Mormons. Several members asked if I would go talk with some of them. On occasion, I did and was well received, but the words which were spoken by me didn't bear any fruit.

✣ THE BEGINNING OF THE LDS MOVEMENT

There are several conflicting versions from Mormon sources. According to one popular Mormon version of their story, the founding of Mormonism began with Joseph Smith's diggings in Palmyra, NY in the year 1820. It was while praying in the woods, that he received his fabled vision of God and Jesus. Three years later, an angel named Moroni appeared at his bedside and claimed to be the son of Mormon. His visitor told him about a book of golden plates that contained the fullness of the everlasting Gospel.

In 1827, in the hill named Cumorah, near Palmyra, NY, Smith unearthed some plates and a pair of large, supernatural spectacles known as the *Urim and Thummim*, which were to be used in translating the hieroglyphics on the plates, which were in a language Smith called "reformed Egyptian."

Smith claimed that during the time he was translating the plates, John the Baptist, who was sent by Peter, James and John, appeared to him and administered a divine ordination and told him to preach a "true" gospel.

With the help of Oliver Cowdery, an itinerant schoolteacher, and Emma Hale, his first and only legal wife, the plates were returned to Moroni after the translation. So, the story goes.

✢ THE BOOK OF MORMON

The *Book of Mormon* was published in 1830 and became the cornerstone of Mormon belief. Smith's *Doctrines and Covenants* and *The Pearl of Great Price* are also considered divine revelations superior to the Bible. They believe these books are superior because they, like Muslims, without a shred of evidence, believe the Bible we have now has been significantly corrupted by Jews and Christians.

When there are conflicts between the Book of Mormon and the Bible, the Book of Mormon takes precedence. On April 6, 1830, Smith, Cowdery, and Smith's brothers, Hyrum and Samuel officially formed the Church of Jesus Christ, now known as the Church of Jesus Christ of Latter-day Saints.

✢ MORMONS ON THE MOVE

Because of their challenge and condemnation of other sects and their polygamous ways, persecutions drove them from New York to Ohio and then to Missouri, where Smith was asked to leave by the governor. After arriving in Nauvoo, IL, Mormons built the largest city in the state.

In conflicts with the law and with charges of treason, Smith and his brother were jailed in 1844.

With a gun which had been smuggled into the jail, Smith shot at his attackers. He was no Jesus. A mob of one hundred or more murdered the two of them. The deaths of these two brothers, insured an instant martyrdom for Joseph Smith. Mormons have acknowledged that Joseph Smith was the husband of forty wives, some as young as fourteen.

In the decade following the death of Joseph Smith, Mormonism split into more than a dozen factions. Problems arose over the choosing of a successor for Smith. Brigham Young was chosen over the objections of others who believed that they were next in line.

During the 1850s, some members parted ways with some of Smith's teaching (especially polygamy) and would later be known as the *Reorganized Church of Jesus Christ of Latter-day Saints.*

The *Reorganized Church of Jesus Christ of Latter-day Saints* would become an American-based international church with headquarters in Independence, MO. In 2001, the name was changed to *The Community of Christ* and today reports 250,000 members in 1,100 congregations in 59 countries.

Brigham Young who was considered by his followers to be a "Modern Moses" moved his majority faction of Mormons from Illinois to Utah in 1847. The biblical Moses led God's people out of Egypt into the promised land. In the 1850s, Young organized the migration of about 16,000 followers who he led into a "land of promise" from Illinois to Utah.

Brigham Young founded Salt Lake City, UT, and became the first governor of the Utah territory. It is reported that he had 55 wives. By divine revelation, polygamy was banned in 1890 when Utah was forced to do so to become a state.

✣ MORMON MEMBERSHIP

Today's Church of Jesus Christ of Latter-day Saints is reported to have 30,500 congregations and a sixteen (16) million plus membership worldwide, six (6) million of these living in the USA. These numbers are questioned by some as to their accuracy. Questionable also, are those who are listed as members, but are not active.

Mormonism is a rapid growing religion, which if present trends continue, could reach 265 million Mormons worldwide by the year 2080.

The Mormon membership is defined as those who are baptized and confirmed; who are under age nine and have been blessed but not baptized; those who are not accountable because of intellectual disabilities regardless of age; and those who are unblessed under age eight when two member parents request it.

✣ MORMONS EVANGELISTIC EFFORTS

A male, when reaching the age of eighteen, is asked to leave their family for two years and dedicate their lives to missionary service. These young men in their missionary work are funded by their families and friends and are to give a minute accounting of their daily activities. They are grouped in two's and neatly attired. You may have seen some in your community.

Those who may have been excused from traveling around the country doing this type of service are required to perform some type of community service or other tasks.

Young women, at the age of nineteen, who are called *"sister missionaries"* are permitted to go on a one year and half year mission but are not required to do so.

Senior couples are encouraged to do some type of ministry: humanitarian efforts, proselytizing and other tasks for the church. For those who are excused, some type of service is still expected.

Members are required to give ten percent of their income to the church. The LDS church is very wealthy. The church owns and manages two different types of business: non-profit and for-profit.

✢ RECOGNIZEABLE MORMONS

The Latter-day Saint members or the church are owners in newspapers, real estate businesses, broadcasting, publishing, media, airlines, hotels and many other businesses which are numerous and visible to modern-day eyes. Deseret Ranches of Florida (Orlando), the largest ranch in Florida, and two hundred thousand acres of land in Utah, are among their holdings.

There are many well-known Mormons from all different walks of life. Some familiar names include: Mitt Romney (U. S. Senator from Utah and former Republican candidate for president); Orin Hatch (former U.S. Senator for 42 years); Harry Reid (former U.S. Senator and Senate Majority leader from 2007-2015); Bill Marriott, (Entrepreneur and Lodging giant); Marie Osmond (Philanthropist, Singer, Actress); Donnie Osmond (Singer, Dancer, Actor); Gladys Knight (Singer, Song Writer, Author, Actress); Stephenie Meyer, (Bestselling Author of The Twilight Book Series); Glenn Beck (Television and Radio giant).

According to a Pew Research poll in 2011, 62% of Mormons said that Americans are uniformed about their religion. If a poll were conducted today among LDS members about their knowledge of LDS, It would probably report a higher percentage of Mormons are truly uninformed about their church. In 2012, Mitt Romney's run for the White House, brought attention to the Church of Jesus Christ of Latter-day Saints.

✣ MORMON LEADERSHIP

Russell M. Nelson, (age 93), has been sustained and set apart as the 17th leader of the Church of Jesus Christ of Latter-day Saints. The churches' symbol is the angel Moroni. He is usually perched atop temple spires with a trumpet in his hand.

The church's hierarchy consists of, the First Presidency (the President and two Counselors), the Quorum of the Twelve Apostles, The First Quorum of the Seventy Stake Presidency, the Ward Bishopric, and lastly, Individual members.

✣ MORMON BELIEFS

The world's population knows very little about the teachings of Mormonism. Brigham Young taught that Adam, was God, who took on a body in the Garden of Eden located in Missouri. One of this Adam-God's wives was Eve. This Adam-God begat Jesus by sexually cohabiting with the Virgin Mary in a physical relationship.

From Young's teachings of polygamy, Mormons received bad publicity. He taught his followers that "the only men who become gods are those who enter into polygamy."

Mormons deny and make modifications to the teachings of Joseph Smith, Brigham Young, and past leaders. Some of their more embarrassing past doctrines such as blood atonement, the Adam-God concept, polygamy, and anti-black beliefs, were taught by men who are still regarded as prophets. Mormonism contradicts, make modifications, and expands on the Holy Word of God. Their belief is that God has not always been the Supreme Being of the Universe but attained this status through righteous living and effort. Accordingly, God is of flesh and blood.

Mormons accept the Christian Bible provided it's correctly translated but give no insights to the verses which are improperly translated. Joseph Smith, who wrote and translated *The Book of Mormon,* believed his writings are more correct than the Holy Bible. His other writings *"Doctrine and Covenants"* and "The Pearl of Great Price," he believed should also take precedence over the Bible.

According to their claims, Mormonism is the only restored, true church, and its concept of salvation must be strictly followed.

✢ THE MORMON HEAVEN

The highest heaven is open only to faithful Mormons who will become gods and join in procreative partnership with God who was once as humans are now. Mormons believe that Jesus is a God, but that men can also become gods.

For Mormons, there are different levels of heaven or kingdoms after physical life: The Celestial Kingdom, The Terrestrial, The Telestial; and Outer Darkness. The final destination for Mormons is determined by what they believe and what they do in this life. Their three levels of heaven teach that only those in the Celestial will live in God's presence. The Christian Bible teaches only one Heaven and one Hell.

✢ PROXY BAPTISMS

The LDS practice Proxy Baptism, which is the living being baptized for those unbaptized who are deceased. Mormons want their deceased family members to be saved even after death. Their justification for Proxy Baptism is found in the Apostle Paul's writing to the Corinthians:

"Now if there is no resurrection, what will those do who are baptized for the dead? If the dead are not raised at all, why are people baptized for them" (1 Cor. 15:29)?

In this passage, Paul is simply pointing out a logical inconsistency in those who baptize for dead they do not believe will rise in a resurrection.

The apostle doesn't give any interpretation to this verse, but this could have been his answer to those who were questioning whether there would be a future resurrection. Why then, were people being baptized for the dead, if there was to be no resurrection?

The Holy Bible is very explicit about a person, while still living, making a personal confession of faith in the Lord Jesus Christ. No one can do that for another person whether alive or dead. There are many passages in the Bible which will testify to a personal relationship being necessary for a person to enter the gates of heaven. One such passage:

"If you declare with your mouth, 'Jesus is Lord,' and believe in your heart that God raised him from the dead, you will be saved. For it is with your heart that you believe and are justified, and it is with your mouth that you profess your faith and are saved" (Rom. 10: 9-10).

✝ MORMON CONFLICTS WITH THE HOLY BIBLE

Mormonism teaches several doctrines which conflicts with Christian beliefs. Some of these from the Word of God are as follows:

"Hear, O Israel: The Lord our God, the Lord is one" (Deut. 6:4).

God has always existed and always will exist: "The eternal God is your refuge" (Deut. 33:27).

God was not created. Instead, God is the Creator: "In the beginning God created the heavens and the earth" (Gen. 1:1).

God is perfect. No one is equal to Him: "Among the gods there is none like you, Lord; no deeds can compare with yours" (Psalm 86:8).

God the Father is not a man: "God is not human, that he should lie, not a human being, that he should change his mind" (Num. 23:19).

God is spirit and spirit is not made of flesh and bone: "God is spirit, and his worshipers must worship in the Spirit and in truth" (John 4:24).

The Latter-day Saints have placed their faith in the teachings of Joseph Smith, Brigham Young and their successors. The *Book of Mormon*, along with other Joseph Smith's volumes (*"Doctrines and Covenants: and "The Pearl of Great Price"*) are believed by Mormons to be superior to the Bible.

If anyone takes words away from the Bible to appease the cultural standards of society, that someone has moved away from the teachings of the Bible.

This has been a lengthy discussion of the LDS movement. Much more could be said about Mormonism as a cult.

CHAPTER FOURTEEN

JEHOVAH'S WITNESSES

THE SOURCES I USED IN RESEARCH OF JEHOVAH'S
Witnesses are Christianity.com, jwfacts.com, 20gramsoul.com,
en.wikipedia.org, answers.com, religionfacts.com, avoidjw.org
and Larson's Book of Cults.

✣ THEIR EVANGELISTIC EFFORTS

My first encounter with members of Jehovah's Witnesses
was in the 1940s. Two women with their literature and
recordings knocked on the front door of our small duplex
in Atlanta. They were cordially greeted by my mother who
invited them to sit down in the swing on our front porch.

Tapes and records were played by them for what appeared
to be hours. Frequent references were made to their version
of the Bible, *The New World Translation*. They were persistent
women. They came again and again for days and weeks until
my mother eventually refused to listen to their beliefs any
further.

My latest and last encounter with Jehovah's Witnesses was
in Rocky Mount, NC in the early years of the 21st century
when two women rang the doorbell of my residence. Opening
the door and extending a greeting, I asked how I could help
them. They never identified themselves as representing any
church but wished to discuss the Bible with me. I wished
them well in the Name of Jesus but told them that I wasn't
interested.

I knew immediately who my visitors were. They were persistent in their efforts to discuss their Bible with me by offering a copy of their magazine *The Watch Tower Announcing Jehovah's Kingdom*. Refusing their magazine and trying to avoid any further discussion, I wished them well again by closing the door as they walked back to their automobile. I passed up a chance to witness to them.

Were they defeated in their efforts to promote their religious movement? No! That was not to be the end of them, for they came back on two other occasions.

Jehovah's Witnesses are well known for their evangelical work by going door to door attempting to make converts. There is reported to be 8.3 million Jehovah's Witnesses around the world with 110,000 to 120,000 congregations in 240 countries where three or more people are gathered to worship weekly. A Pew Research Center Religious Landscape Study in 2014 reported a 2.5 million membership in the USA.

Only Jehovah's Witnesses who actively preach the good news of God's Kingdom at least one hour each month are counted. Members of this sect earnestly seek to win others to their beliefs.

✦ JEHOVAH'S WITNESSES' FOUNDER

The Jehovah's Witnesses was founded in 1879 by Charles Taze Russell, an American Restorationist minister, in Pittsburgh PA. The movement originated from Mr. Russell's Bible studies classes which were later identified as the Millennial Dawn Bible Study.

From these teachings in the 1870s, Mr. Russell began to dispute some of the traditional views within Christianity and his beliefs would later become the forerunner of what is now known as Jehovah's Witnesses. It was after the death of Mr. Russell in 1916, that the movement in 1931 under the direction of John Rutherford became known as Jehovah's Witnesses.

✣ JEHOVAH'S WITNESSES AS CITIZENS

What do Jehovah's Witnesses believe? They have numerous beliefs: their refusal to accept blood transfusions under extraordinary conditions; a refusal to donate vital organs; to receive transplants; and celebrating birthdays are not things done "as citizens." Add to these a refusal to vote, run for public office, participate in lobbying or action to change the government, salute the flag, sing *The Star-Spangled Banner* and a refusal to serve in the Armed Forces. Jehovah's Witnesses don't observe Christmas, Easter or nationalistic holidays.

✣ JEHOVAH'S WITNESSES RELIGIOUS BELIEFS

Jehovah's Witnesses are also errant concerning biblical matters: Jehovah's Witnesses do not believe in the Trinity; the Holy Spirit is an impersonal force of God and not a living person of the Trinity; Jesus was Jehovah's first creation and was Michael the archangel; Jesus was not God in the flesh, but was a perfect man; Jesus rose as a spirit, but did not bodily rise from the dead; Jesus returned to earth invisibly in 1914; only Jehovah's Witnesses will be saved; good works are necessary for salvation; there is no hell of fire for the unsaved; the soul 'sleeps' at death and does not immediately go to heaven; only 144,000 Jehovah's Witnesses will go to heaven; the other members of their faith will live on the new earth; and the cross should not be used by followers of God since it's a pagan symbol.

✢ JEHOVAH'S WITNESSES' BIBLE

Jehovah's Witnesses have their own translation of the Bible *the New World Translation* (NWT) was released at a Jehovah's Witnesses' Convention in Yankee Stadium on August 2, 1950. It included only the New Testament. The NWT was issued in stages and volumes during the 1950s before the completion of both the New Testament and Old Testament in 1961.

Before they purchased the rights in 1902 to the Emphatic Diaglott New Testament, they used the Greber translation (he was a spirit medium), and appealed to a variety of versions employing whichever one they could twist to support their doctrine and the translation of the NWT, the King James Version was used. Many words and passages are purposely mistranslated in the NWT to align with Jehovah's Witnesses' beliefs. An example is their translation of the Gospel of John, chapter 1, verse 1:

> In the beginning was the Word, and the Word was with God, and the Word was God.

Their translation of *"God"* reads *"a god."*

The Jehovah's Witnesses parent organization, The Watchtower Society, claims their translation of the Holy Scriptures was made directly from Hebrew, Aramaic and Greek into modern-day English by a committee of anointed Jehovah's Witnesses. (The names of these translators have been kept secret due to beliefs by some that the translators were not knowledgeable of Hebrew, Aramaic and Greek). Bill Cetnar named them. They have almost zero credentials. The NWT came years after Mr. Russell's death who claimed that he knew Greek and Hebrew, but later testified under oath that he did not.

No other religious group uses *The New World Translation* and Jehovah's Witnesses make little use of other Bibles except in witnessing to Christians for which they are taught how to twist and criticize the King James.

✛ JEHOVAH'S WITNESSES EVENTS OVER THE YEARS

1879: The publishing of *Zion's Watch Tower* and *Herald of Christ's Presence magazine*.

1881: Zion's Watch Tower Tract Society, was incorporated in 1884.

1886: Russell begins the writing of *Studies in the Scriptures* which came to be considered second only to the Bible in importance. (Actually, Russell claimed more important.)

1908: Moved its headquarters from Pittsburgh to New York.

1914: The year designated (prediction) by Mr. Russell for Christ's visible second coming. His visible return was changed to invisible after the failure. Also, the world's end has been prophesied for 1918, 1920, 1925, 1941, and even as late as 1975.

1916: After the death of Mr. Russell, Joseph Franklin Rutherford, who was not chosen by Mr. Russell before his death, succeeded causing some controversy.

1925: Predicted by Mr. Rutherford as the year that Abraham, Isaac, Jacob and the prophets would return to earth.

1931: Still under the leadership of Mr. Rutherford, using the word *"witnesses"* from Isaiah 43:10, the name *"Jehovah's Witnesses"* was adopted.

1942: Joseph Franklin Rutherford dies and was succeeded by Nathan Homer Knorr.

1975: Armageddon was predicted and was derived from a calculation of Adam's creation plus 6,000 years. The failure of this prediction was explained by saying that it was Eve, who came months or years later than Adam, from which the calculation should have been made.

1977: Nathan Homer Knorr die, and Frederick Franz became his successor.

1993: Milton Henschel succeeded Franz.

✢ JEHOVAH'S WITNESSES' LEADERSHIP

The Watchtower Society is reputed to be the authority of Jehovah's Witnesses. L. Weaver, Jr. is the current president of the Watchtower Society.

Ask the membership of Jehovah's Witnesses who is the leader of Jehovah's Witnesses and they will tell you that Jesus Christ is the Head of their movement. But that is far from the truth since Jesus has been stripped of his identity. Jehovah's Witnesses do not consider Jesus to be Eternal God, and the Creator of the universe, which is declared in the following verses from the Christian's Holy Bible:

> For we do not have a high priest who is unable to empathize with our weaknesses, but we have one who has been tempted in every way, just as we are - yet he did not sin (Heb. 4:15).

> For in Christ all the fullness of the Deity lives in bodily form, and in Christ you have been brought to fullness. He is the head over every power and authority (Col. 2: 9-10).

✢ JEHOVAH'S WITNESSES' STRUCTURE

The Governing Body is a group of men that provide direction for Jehovah's Witnesses' worldwide activities. This group makeup is composed of eight men who make attempts to deny that they are leaders.

This Governing Body explains away their leadership by using two verses from the New Testament.

> But I want you to realize that the head of every man is Christ, and the head of the woman is man, and the head of Christ is God (1 Cor. 11:3).

> For the husband is the head of the wife as Christ is the head of the church, his body, of which he is the Savior (Eph. 5:23).

These two verses which are listed here from the Holy Bible do very little to justify their attempt to explain away their leadership.

Since 1976, the governing body has established six committees to oversee various aspects of Jehovah's Witnesses' work and the work of the governing body themselves.

The eight men from the Governing Body, which are called *helpers,* have been assigned to the below listed committees. Each member of the governing body serves on one or more of these six committees.

✛ COMMITTEES AND THEIR PURPOSES

1. THE COORDINATOR'S COMMITTEE: Supervises legal matters, responds to disasters and aids Jehovah's Witnesses who are persecuted for their beliefs.

2. THE PERSONNEL COMMITTEE: Oversees the arrangements of Bethel which is the name of local, regional and worldwide headquarters family members and staff.

3. THE PUBLISHING COMMITTEE: Supervises the production and shipping of religious literature and the construction of meeting places, translation offices and branch facilities.

4. THE SERVICE COMMITTEE: Oversees Jehovah's Witnesses' work of preaching the good news about how God is going to destroy the whole world so that a few million members can live in perfect peace.

5. THE TEACHING COMMITTEE: Directs the preparation of spiritual instructions provided by means of meetings, schools, and audio and video programs.

6. THE WRITING COMMITTEE: Directs the preparation of spiritual instruction provided in printed and electronic form and oversees the translation work for their books and magazines.

Jehovah's Witnesses have 87 Branch offices worldwide. Each of these Branch offices is referred to as *"Bethel."*

Much more could be written and said about Jehovah's Witnesses. You may have already had one to knock at your door, and you may have experienced their teachings. If not, your doorbell or a knock at any minute could announce their arrival. And, when they come, there will be two of them.

CHAPTER FIFTEEN

BIBLE-BELIEVING CHRISTIAN DENOMINATIONS

AMONG PROTESTANTS, THERE ARE MANY denominations: Methodists, Baptists, Church of Christ, Church of God, Episcopal, Presbyterians, Lutherans, etc. One could list page after page of many other denominations. And, one could list page after page of different types of Baptists, Methodists, Lutherans, etc. All denominations believe they are right with their interpretation of the Word of God. Even in small communities, there are churches everywhere. For the populace it becomes a menu: pick and choose the denomination which is nearest to your beliefs.

Be aware that there are many Baptist churches. There are two well-known Baptist Groups: The Southern Baptists and American Baptists. There are over two hundred identified different kinds of Baptists in America. To name a few, there are Regular Baptists, Primitive Baptists, United Baptist; Free Will Baptists; Separate Baptists; Two Seed-in-the-Spirit Predestination Baptists, Seventh Day Baptists, Duck River Baptists and Independent Baptists. The listing of Baptists is long. Their beliefs and practices vary widely.

Over the ages, not only Baptists, but other denominations as well, have split and gone separate ways. Some are accused of getting their Bible and starting another church if they don't like their pastor. It is also said about the pastor, "if he can't get along with his congregation, he takes some members with him and starts his own church."

The Lord God isn't happy with Christians and their disagreements. Many believe that they are doing it for the Lord. The grumbling is within us.

The Roman Catholic Church believes they are the true Church, stemming from their belief that the Apostle Peter was their first Pope. It is highly unlikely that Peter was the leader of the church in Jerusalem, since the Book of Acts (Chapter 15) identifies James, the half-brother of Jesus, as the one who was in authority.

When churches quote from the Apostle's Creed "I believe in the Holy Catholic Church," they are speaking of the Universal Church, not the Roman Catholic Church. The Apostle's Creed is repeated each Sunday throughout the world by many denominations, especially Methodists.

I have served in Baptist churches and in one Methodist church. I was surprised when a Methodist minister asked me to serve as his associate at a local United Methodist church in a small town in Alabama. It will never happen were my thoughts since I was a Baptist and had attended a Baptist Seminary. Furthermore, approval would have to come from a bishop in that area. Nevertheless, I was approved.

I must confess that the only reason I was attending a Methodist church was because my wife was a Methodist, and her father, mother, and sister were Methodists. But I was still a Baptist and would remain a Baptist in beliefs. I didn't agree with their interpretation of sprinkling the head for baptism, nor their belief in having to perform good deeds as part of their continued salvation.

I met many Christians in that congregation. It's not denominations that make Christians. It's the blood of Jesus Christ, who died on a cruel Roman Cross, that saves each of us from our sins.

The interpretation of the Bible is one of the issues which keeps denominations apart or separate. There is only one Lord, one Faith, one Baptism. And Jesus is our Lord.

In 2013, the membership statistics of the ten largest denominational groups in the United States were this: The Southern Baptist Convention, 16.2 million; United Methodist Church, 7.8 million; The Church of God in Christ, 5.5 million; National Baptist Convention, 5.0 million; Evangelical Lutheran Church, USA, 4.5 million; National Baptist Convention of America, 3.5 million; Assemblies of God, 2.9 million; Presbyterian Church (USA), 2.8 million; African Methodist Episcopal Church, 2.5 million; and National Missionary Baptist Convention of America, 2.5 million. These figures are estimates reported by churches to their respective conventions. Membership within all Protestant denominations in the United States is estimated to be 800 million.

In the next three chapters, I will highlight what is happening in the Roman Catholic Church, and two Protestant denominational groups: In the Southern Baptist Convention and the United Methodist Church. These three bodies lead all other USA churches in membership. There are sexual scandals in two of these bodies and the other denomination is considering dividing into three possible groupings.

Over many years, these three church bodies have been very influential in reaching people for Christ. According to current statistics, these three bodies are on the decline. Should present trends continue, their influence among the populace will dwindle and fade. Their continuing failure to reach the unsaved will contribute to **THE KILLING OF THE CHRISTIAN CHURCH IN AMERICA.**

CHAPTER SIXTEEN

THE ROMAN CATHOLIC CHURCH

THE CHURCH AT ROME BELIEVES THAT ITS FIRST POPE dates-back-to the Apostle Peter, who, being asked by Jesus as to who he (Jesus) was, replied, "You are the Messiah, the Son of the Living God."

> Jesus replied, "Blessed are you, Simon son of Jonah, for this was not revealed to you by flesh and blood, but by my Father in heaven, And I tell you that you are Peter, and on this rock I will build my church, and the gates of Hades will not overcome it. I will give you the keys of the kingdom of heaven; whatever you bind on earth will be bound in heaven, and whatever you loose on earth will be loosed in heaven" (Matt. 16: 16-19).

The Roman Catholic Church interprets this passage to mean that Saint Peter was the first Pope. Protestant churches, however, don't interpret this passage of Scripture to mean that only upon this Apostle was this privilege given. It is interpreted by the Protestants as saying: "Upon the Christ-like-faith that is expressed by Peter, Jesus will build his church." There are numerous Protestant views of this passage.

The Apostle Peter had the faith to profess Jesus. And, so does every person who has God-given faith to believe that Jesus is the Messiah, the Son of the Living God. This God-given faith and confession enable each-and-every believer to enter the kingdom of God. Peter, being an outspoken one and a leader of the twelve disciples, was speaking not only for himself, but for the other apostles who had God-given faith.

Books, commentaries, and concordances fill many library's shelves with the interpretations of these verses of Scripture. Only God builds his invisible church. It is by Jesus' death and resurrection and the faith given by God to each person expressing this faith that we enter His kingdom.

According to a Pew Survey in 2014, the percentage of United States Roman Catholics has dropped from previous surveys, and Catholicism is losing members faster than any Protestant denomination. A report by the Pew Forum found that the total number of Catholics in the United States has dropped by 3 million since 2007 and now comprise only about 20 percent or one fifth of the total population.

The 2014 Pew Report disclosed that for every Catholic convert in the USA, more than six Catholics leave the Roman Catholic Church. The Catholic Church, therefore, is losing more members than it gains at a higher rate than any Protestant denomination with nearly 13 percent of all Americans describing themselves as being former Catholics.

Rhode Island has the highest per capita Catholic population in the United States at 44 percent. There are other Northeastern states which have percentages above 30 percent. These states are Connecticut, Massachusetts, New Jersey and New York. Mississippi has the lowest per capita Catholic population at just 4 percent. The church's makeup is 54 percent women and 59 percent white.

According to a Pew Center survey in 2010, the United States is home to about 7 percent of all Catholics in the world. A 2010 survey listed 75.4 million Catholics living in the USA, and 22 million of these were born outside the United States. Slightly more that 13 percent of the overall US population of Catholics is foreign born.

✢ MARTIN LUTHER

There are numerous disagreements of the teachings of the Roman Catholic Church and those of Protestant denominations. Here are some things to know:

Martin Luther, a German priest and professor of Theology, is credited with being the founder of the Protestant Reformation. The Lutheran churches today have many different bodies, all of which base their teachings and practices to some degree on the work of Luther.

Martin Luther nailed his 95 Theses to the door at Wittenberg's Castle Church on October 31, 1517.

His 95 Theses expressed his growing concern with the corruption within the Roman Catholic Church and were a call for a full reform of the Catholic Church.

Pope Leo X excommunicated Luther from the Church and openly expressed a desire that Luther be killed. While in hiding, Luther produced a translation of the Bible into the German language.

In 1529, some twelve years after the nailing of his 95 Theses, the word "Protestant," which described those who were in support of Luther's protests, became a popular term. His 95 Theses was a document listing various oppressive and unbiblical doctrines and practices of the Roman Catholic Church.

Luther questioned the sale of indulgences purported to absolve sinners. His emphasis was on the authority of the Bible and salvation by grace through faith. Luther recognized that only God's grace, not good works, could save him.

Martin Luther died in 1546 with his revolutionary 95 Theses forming the foundation for what is known today as the Protestant Reformation.

✣ PURGATORY

Catholicism's term for a "temporary state of suffering and purification for believers who die in a state of sin is "Purgatory." The Catholic Church teaches that all those in "Purgatory" or "a cleansing place," can eventually go to heaven. Purgatory is the location of one's intermediate state after physical death in which those destined for heaven undergo purification, so-as-to achieve the holiness necessary to enter the joy of heaven."

Purgatory is generally not shared by other branches of Christianity. Catholics point to the Book of Maccabees as their justification. The books of Maccabees were in most Protestant Bibles including the 1611 KJV, until fairly-recently. They are not included in Bibles which are used by Protestant church members today and is not believed to be biblical. These books are part of the group of scriptural books of Apocrypha, which are not considered scriptural by Protestants.

Church members are encouraged to burn candles, to pray, and to give money so that their love ones can transcend from *Purgatory* into their final bliss. This is an area in which Martin Luther and other priests took an issue.

✣ HOLY COMMUNION OR THE HOLY EUCHARIST

The Roman Catholic Church refuses Holy Eucharist to their members for the reasons listed below. (In some of these areas there may be exceptions if reasons will justify them.)

* Receiving or participating in an abortion.
* Engaging in homosexual acts.
* Having sexual intercourse outside of marriage or in an invalid marriage.

* Deliberately engaging in impure thoughts.
* Not having been to confession since one's last mortal sin.
* Not having abstained from food and drink at least for one hour prior to Holy Communion.
* It is necessary for members to believe in the doctrine of transubstantiation. The term, "transubstantiation" is used to the belief that the bread and wine used in the Holy Eucharist, are transformed into the actual body, blood and divinity of Christ.

The Catholic Church's justification for the exclusion of some from this sacrament are these words from the Bible:

> Jesus said to them, "Very truly I tell you, unless you eat the flesh of the Son of Man and drink his blood, you have no life in you. Whoever eats my flesh and drinks my blood has eternal life, and I will raise them up at the last day. For my flesh is real food and my blood is real drink. Whoever eats my flesh and drinks my blood remains in me, and I in them'" (John 6: 53-56).

* A person must not be under an ecclesiastical censure.
* Non-Catholics and other denominations.

It is devastating for a member of the Roman Catholic Church to be excluded from Holy Communion or to be excommunicated. The most common cause of excommunication is abortion. Another grave sin is leaving the Catholic Church and joining a Protestant denomination or leaving the church and not joining anything.

✢ SEXUAL ABUSES AND CORRUPTION

The following article by the Associated Press and written by Regina Garcia Cano and David Crary, is titled, *"U. S.*

Catholic Bishops Convene to Confront Sex-abuse Crisis" appeared in the Rocky Mount Telegram (NC) in the summer of 2019.

"The nation's Roman Catholic bishops convened a high-stakes meeting on Tuesday under pressure to confront the ever-widening child sexual abuse crisis that has disillusioned many churchgoers.

A key question at the four-day gathering: How willing are the bishops to give lay experts a major role in holding the clergy accountable?

Francesco Cesareo, an academic who chairs a national sex-abuse review board set up by the bishops, told the meeting's opening session that the involvement of laity is critical if the bishops are to regain public trust after 'a period of intense suffering' for the church.

He said the review board 'remains uncomfortable with allowing bishops to review allegation against other bishops—this essentially means bishops policing bishops.'

'We find ourselves at a turning point, a critical moment in our history, which will determine in many ways the future vibrancy of the church and whether or not trust in your leadership can be restored,' *Cesareo said.*

The deliberations will be guided by a new law that Pope Francis issued on May 9. It requires priests and nuns worldwide to report sexual abuse as well as correction by their superiors to church authorities. It also calls for allegations against bishops to be reported to the Vatican and a supervisory bishop.

Among the many agenda items in Baltimore is a proposal to create an independent, third-party entity that would review allegations of abuse. Cesareo has said all abuse-related allegations concerning bishops should be reported to civil authorities first and then to a review board.

A national survey released on Tuesday by the Pew Research Center illustrates the extent of disenchantment among U.S. Catholics. The March poll found about one-fourth of Catholics saying they had scaled back Mass attendance and reduced donations because of the abuse crisis, and only 30% said U.S. bishops had done a good or excellent job in responding.

According to the Center for Applied Research in the Apostolate, an authoritative source of Catholic related date, 45% of U.S. Catholics attended Mass at least once a month in 2018, down from 57% in 1990.

According to the center's estimates, there were 76.8 million Catholics in the United States last year, down from 81.2 million in 2005. It remains the largest denomination in the country."

Many practices of the Roman Catholic Church are not Bible-based. Members are not encouraged to read the Holy Bible and to discern the truths. Priests are considered as *"fathers"* to which a member comes to be absolved of his or her sins. The Pope is its leader and is revered as its authority. Many (especially US) Catholics ignore the Pope and a host of issues. The authority rests entirely in the directions which comes from the Vatican.

A lengthy article written by Michael Rezendes of the Associated Press and titled *"Lawsuit:* Famed Jesuit Abused Boy

1,000 Times Around the World" was printed in the Rocky Mount (NC)Telegram on January 2, 2020. A few quotes from this article are as follows:

> "In the nearly two decades since the clergy abuse scandal erupted, thousands of survivors have stepped forward to tell their painful stories. Hundreds more revealed their abuse in lawsuits earlier this year, when the state of New York opened a one-year window that allows survivors to file child sex abuse lawsuits without regard to the statute of limitations. And hundreds more, including Goldberg, are expected to step forward as a similar window opens Jan. 1, (2020) in California.
>
> But many victims still suffer in silence, often taking decades to step forward if they ever do. Advocates say that Catholic priests, as representatives of God and respected members of their communities, often are able to exert control over the children they target, especially when they are helping the child or their families overcome poverty or other obstacles."

The above article is one of untold numbers which could be written about the abuse of children by the clergy. The Roman Catholic Church has much to do in addressing its problems of sexual abuse by members of its clergy.

The sexual abuse by Roman Catholic clergy has been placed on the backburner for untold ages.

CHAPTER SEVENTEEN

SOUTHERN BAPTIST CONVENTION CHURCHES (SBC)

THE FOLLOWING BRIEF HISTORY OF THE BAPTIST movement comes from a research of the Learn Religions website and various other resources:

Southern Baptist history dates to the Reformation in England in the 16th Century.

One prominent reformer in the early 17th century, John Smyth was a strong promotor in adult baptism. In 1609 he rebaptized himself and others. Smyth's reforms birthed the first English Baptist Church.

Roger Williams came to America to escape religious persecution. In 1638, he established the First Baptist Church in America in Providence, Rhode Island.

By the mid-eighteenth century, the number of Baptists increased greatly as a result of the Great Awakening pioneered by Jonathan Edwards.

In 1755, Shubael Stearns began to spread his Baptist beliefs in North Carolina. The North Carolina Baptists or Stubael followers were referred to as separate Baptists. The Regular Baptists resided primarily in the North.

By the 1830s, tension began to mount between Northern and Southern Baptists. One issue that severely divided the Baptists was slavery. As a result of this division, Baptists in the South met in 1845 and organized the Southern Baptist Convention.

From 1845 to 1891 the Southern Baptist Convention continued to use materials from the American Baptist Publication Society in Philadelphia, PA. In 1891, Lifeway was named the Sunday School Board of SBC Sunday Board and was headquartered in Nashville, TN.

✥ A DECLINING MEMBERSHIP

In recent years, the membership of the SBC has been on the decline. At one time there were over seventeen million members. As of 2018, the SBC reported a membership of 15,005,638 with an average weekly attendance of 5,320,488. Annual baptisms reported by the forty-seven thousand churches were 254,122.

In 1948, there were six million members in the SBC. In 2013, 16.2 million were claimed by the SBC within the United States.

The focus on evangelism or reaching people for Christ Jesus began its decline in the SBC in the latter part of the 1960s. Today, there are approximately seven and one-half billion people on earth. Christian churches and especially the SBC have not kept up with the population growth even though there are more methods to reach people which are now available.

An inventory of your church roll will reveal that it contains the names of some who have moved away and have joined other churches by their personal statements. Some members never attend church and prefer staying at home. Only about thirty (30) percent of members on a churches' roll attend on a regular basis or are active participants.

Some churches refuse to monitor their church rolls. Members which they have not seen or heard from in a very long time remain on their rolls. The accuracy of a church's membership roll is doubtful.

Current membership figures from the 47,000 autonomous churches indicate a membership of 14 million plus members. The Southern Baptist Convention is considered the largest Protestant denomination in the United States. Over half of all Southern Baptists in the world live in five southern states: Texas, Georgia, North Carolina, Tennessee, and Alabama.

The state of Texas has had the largest representation of elected SBC presidents with 12, followed by Georgia with nine and Tennessee with seven.

The SBC operates six seminaries which are listed in the order of their founding: Southern Baptist Theological Seminary, Louisville, KY (1859); Southwestern Baptist Theological, Fort Worth, TX (1908); New Orleans Baptist Theological Seminary, New Orleans, LA (1917); Golden Gate Baptist Theological Seminary, Mill Valley, CA (1944); Southeastern Baptist Theological Seminary, Wake Forest, NC (1951) and Midwestern Baptist Theological Seminary, Kansas City, MO (1957)

The president of the Southern Baptist Convention is elected or reelected at the annual convention each year. Some of the following presidents will be recognizable by the reader:

> Robert Greene Lee, elected 1948 and 1949, served as pastor of Bellevue Baptist Church, Memphis, TN. Dr. Lee was noted for his sermon, *"Payday Someday,"* which he preached in various cities throughout the United States.

> James David Grey (1951 and 1952), First Baptist Church, New Orleans, LA.

> Herschel Harold Hobbs, (1961 and 1962) First Baptist Church, Oklahoma City, OK.

> Wallie Amos Criswell, (1968 and 1969) First Baptist Church, Dallas.

Adrian Rogers, (1979, 1986, 1987) Bellevue Baptist Church, Memphis.

Charles Frazier Stanley, (1984, 1985) First Baptist Church, Atlanta.

Fred Luter, Jr., (2012, 2013) New Orleans, LA. The first person of color.

✢ TODAY'S SOUTHERN BAPTISTS

The current president of the Southern Baptist Convention is J. D. Greear, who is pastor of The Summit Church in Raleigh-Durham, NC. He was reelected to the office in June 2019.

Southern Baptist churches are autonomous. They hire and fire their staff members.

Each church decides the amount which is contributed to their state's mission boards and to the cooperative fund for evangelistic efforts of reaching people throughout the United States and worldwide.

The Southern Baptist Convention is reportedly a very evangelistic and conservative group. It does not believe in having female pastors in their pulpits. However, there are some churches which are more liberal and deviate from this.

During the American Civil Rights Movement in the 1950s and 1960s, the SBC took no active role, and in some locales, strongly opposed racial equality.

In 1995, on the 150th anniversary of the founding of the SBC, at its national meeting in Atlanta, SBC leaders adopted a resolution on racial reconciliation. The resolution condemned racism and acknowledged the SBC's role in supporting slavery and affirmed the equality of all people on scriptural grounds. Further, it apologized to African

Americans, asking their forgiveness, and pledging to eradicate all forms of racism from Southern Baptist life.

Recently, I watched a traditional service from a Southern Baptist Church, where an associate pastor, a woman, filled the pulpit in the absence of the senior pastor. Had I not known that it was a Baptist Church, I would have believed that I was watching a Methodist service. There were many similarities to Methodism-like the saying of the Lord's Prayer and the Apostle's Creed by this church every Sunday.

A few areas in need of addressing within the SBC are Calvinism, a growing liberalism and sexual abuse by the clergy.

✢ CALVINISM BEING PREACHED IN MANY SBC CHURCHES

Among some Southern Baptist pastors and seminaries, the teachings of 16th-century Reformer John Calvin are increasingly becoming more prominent. Calvinism teaches that when Jesus died on the cross, it was only for humans whom God had elected to save and not for everyone.

Calvin's doctrine of predestination is that a person's salvation has already been determined. This teaching will appear to some, that there isn't the need for a gospel message of salvation to be preached since a person's salvation has already been determined. This doctrine can be an excuse which the clergy may use when baptisms are not happening. In other words, God's predestination is not available to some lost souls within the assembly.

It is estimated that 30% of churches within the SBC have Calvinistic leanings. Invitations at the conclusion of a worship service have been done away with in some SBC churches.

Calvinist leaning preachers, if confronted by their parishioners about their beliefs, might call for a confidence vote or just leave, taking with them their Calvinists followers. Churches have by-laws which state the approval level needed by a minister to remain. If the confidence vote for a pastor is less than that which is required in the by-laws, pastors are either fired or forced to resign. Some pastors will go peacefully, while others do not.

✢ A Social Gospel Being Preached in Many SBC Churches

Many SBC churches are becoming more liberal. Baptisms and the retention of members are on a downward whirl. People are not walking the aisle to receive Jesus and numerous churches are not growing.

All to often a socialistic type ministry has become the norm. Messages of *"Loving Thy Neighbor"* and how to live good and prosperous lives are taught by some *teaching* pastors. Preaching to the lost is placed on the back burner and will remain there until God called *preaching* ministers fill the pulpits. Thousands of these 47,000 churches have strayed from the ministry of reaching the lost.

✢ Sexual Abuse by The Clergy and Staff Members in SBC Churches

For decades the public has been hearing about the sexual abuse within the Roman Catholic Church. Since the #MeToo movement took wings, SBC sexual abuse survivors have been coming forth with their stories, which may date back 20 years or more. Assuming all claims are valid, seven hundred (700) victims within SBC churches have been left without apologies or justice.

The Southern Baptist Convention, due to articles appearing in the Houston Chronicle and San Antonio

Express-News, is being pressured to take steps to confront this problem. It was an issue addressed at the SBC 2019 annual meeting in Birmingham.

In 2018 at the Southern Baptist Convention in Dallas, the newly elected president, J. D. Greear, formed an advisory group to draft recommendations on how to deal with this spreading scandal. This nine- member team includes a psychologist, a former prosecutor, an attorney, a detective, and Rachael Denhollander, who was the first woman to go public with charges against Larry Nassar, the sports doctor.

Little has been done in the past to train clergy and staff on how to confront this situation. Problems include the failure to believe and support victims, the failure to report abuse to law enforcement agencies, and the recommending suspected perpetrators to new employment. At the Southern Baptist Theological Seminary in Wake Forest, NC, it was reported that the seminary president encouraged a rape victim to not report the incident to authorities and to forgive her abuser.

Consideration is now being given by the SBC to a training curriculum to be used at churches and seminaries to improve responses to abuse. They are employing database listings of sex abusers and background checks of church leaders.

The flaming fire of a once vibrant evangelistic denomination is flickering.

CHAPTER EIGHTEEN

UNITED METHODIST CHURCH (UMC)

JOHN WESLEY, BORN IN 1703, CHARLES, (HIS BROTHER,) and George Whitefield are the founders of the Methodist movement.

John Wesley was ordained a priest in the Church of England in 1728. He would remain an Anglican preacher until his death.

It was at Oxford that John Wesley joined a group which he would later lead. This group also included his brother Charles. Because of this group's 'methodical devotion and study,' its members became known as Methodists. This 18th century movement sought to reform The Church of England. Later, George Whitefield, at the invitation of Charles, would join the group

In 1735, as priests in the Church of England, John and Charles Wesley left England for Georgia in the American colonies. John Wesley became the pastor of a church in Savannah. This was the beginning of the Methodist movement in America in the years of 1735 and 1736.

Experiencing some difficulties with his members over Communion and other matters, John Wesley, disillusioned and spiritually low, returned to England.

John Wesley expressed his feelings of despair to Peter Boehler, a Moravian, who encouraged him to attend one of their meetings. At a Moravian service on May 24, 1738, John Wesley felt his "heart strangely warmed." "I felt that I did trust in Christ, Christ alone, for salvation, and an assurance was given me that He had taken away my sins, even mine, and saved me from the law of sin and death."

George Whitefield invited John Wesley to join him in his evangelistic ministry in the late 1730s. Whitefield was an outdoor preacher, something almost unthought of at that time. These two would later disagree over Whitefield's Calvinistic beliefs of predestination. Wesley, believing in the Free Grace which was afforded by God to everyone, was strongly opposed to Whitefield's beliefs. Whitefield was more the evangelistic one while John Wesley was the older one and more the organizer and sustainer of the Methodist movement.

United Methodist Churches were created on April 23, 1968 when the Evangelical United Brethren Church and the Methodist Church united to form a new denomination.

✢ MAKEUP OF THE UMC

The United Methodist Church (UMC) is organized as a hierarchical system with the highest level being the General Conference which speaks for the United Methodist Church. The next levels are Jurisdictional and Central Conferences composed of annual conferences. These annual conferences are divided into Districts.

The churches in the UMC are "owned in trust" by the trustees of each local church. Local church trustees cannot sell the building and use the funds to transfer to an independent church. They cannot leave the UMC and make the active church an independent church. Should the local trustees choose to close the church, the property is turned over to the Conference trustee board. UMC property is the property in trust of the Annual Conference and cannot be given or sold without Conference approval.

UMC ministers are appointed by bishops who appoint ministers to serve for varying periods of time. The pastor is not a member of the church to which he is appointed. The bishop is the primary pastor of each local church.

The Bible, Book of Discipline of the United Methodist Church and the Twenty-five articles of Religion are used. John Westley's ultimate intention for his Methodist movement was devout godliness.

United Methodists claim worldwide membership to be eleven million or more. Membership in the United States is at eight million, making it the second largest denomination in America

✝ CRISIS WITHIN THE UNITED METHODIST CHURCH

The United Methodist Church for some years has been divided over the issue of same sex marriages and the ordaining of LGBTQ clergy.

At a recent February 2019 conference in St. Louis, UMC officials and lay members voted to strengthen prohibitions and to ban LGBTQ people from being ordained and ministers from performing same-sex weddings within the church.

For several years, the LGBTQ movement and their supporters within the church have been pushing to allow persons of any sexual orientation to be married in the church and for gays to participate in leadership roles.

In some areas, churches are already in violation of their Book of Discipline teachings by the appointing of gay ministers and the performing of same-sex marriages. A lesbian pastor, Karen Oliveto, was elected a bishop in the church. Same-sex marriages were happening.

The denomination's bishops, prior to a February 2019 meeting, proposed a resolution for the "One Church Plan" which would allow for local congregations, conferences and clergy to make their own choices about same-sex marriages and the ordination of LGBTQ pastors.

In the February 2019 meeting, "The Traditional Plan" which was designed to strengthen the denomination's teaching against homosexuality, was approved. This plan would uphold the denomination's Book of Discipline which does not allow for same sex marriages and for self- avowed practicing homosexuals to be ordained.

✢ UMC DOING THEIR OWN THING

The membership of the UMC in the United States consists of three groups which are cataloged as follows: The Traditionalist or Conservatives, which lean to the ultimate authority of the Scriptures, the Moderate or Centrists Moderate and lastly, the Progressives or Liberals.

There is a scheduled meeting in the year 2020 which will attempt resolutions to this matter. Presently, the UMC is on the verge of splitting into three different denominations.

In an article written by Kristi Sturgill of the Associated Press, which appeared in newspapers in July 2019, she writes about the February 2019 meeting among Methodists. Here are some of her thoughts about what was happening in the Charlotte area:

> "UMC churches in Charlotte, NC span different views, some fully supporting LGBTQ marriage and others maintaining that it's sinful. Self-identifying 'progressive' churches say God's love and inclusion call them to fully accept LGBTQ marriage and clergy. Self-proclaimed 'traditional' churches say including LGBTQ identifying congregants does not mean supporting their marriage."

In the months following the February ruling, many conferences and churches have quietly or openly opposed the decision. Some Charlotte pastors married LGBTQ couples before the ruling. Rev. Valerie Rosenquist and Rev. Michelle Chappell, lead pastors of First United Methodist Church and Dilworth United Methodist Church respectively, say they're open to doing it again."

✢ CONSEQUENCES AND OWNERSHIP

At the February 2019 conference, there were consequences identified for any disobedience to the Traditional Plan, which would become effective on January 1, 2020. For the first offense to this plan, clergy would be suspended without pay for one year. For a second offense, clergy would lose their credentials.

Ms. Sturgill in her Associated Press article stated further, *"At a conference in June (2019), the Western North Carolina Conference officially rejected the Traditional Plan. However, that decision does not change the consequences for marrying LGBTQ couples."*

From the information given by the Associated Press writer, it appears that some UMC churches in the Charlotte area are completely opposed to the Traditional Plan. Yet, there are United Methodist Churches who affirm and agree with the Plan in the Charlotte area. Among these are comments from the clerical staff at Good Shepherd Church. *"The staff at Good Shepherd Church felt peaceful and clear that the Bible forbids LGBTQ marriage,"* Davis said.

"They don't think it is God's design." "Jesus affirms heterosexual marriage. God has already decided," said Brooke Presley, their children's ministry leader.

Opposition to the Traditional Plan isn't in Charlotte alone. The vote at the February 2019 meeting came from delegates across these USA.

It will be very difficult for some churches to leave the United Methodist Church since Local churches' property and buildings belong to the bishops. Some Methodist churches are considering the removal of the word "United" from their name.

The membership of the United Methodist Church outside the United States falls within the beliefs of the Traditional or Conservatives group in the USA and to be totally against homosexuality.

The LGBTQ movement is moving not only within the United Methodist Church, but within other churches in America and worldwide.

A more recent article from the Associated Press and which appeared in *The Rocky Mount Telegram* on January 4, 2020, and titled, "Methodists Propose Amicable Split states:

> "United Methodist Church leaders from around the world and across ideological divides unveiled a plan Friday for a new conservative denomination that would split from the church in an-attempt-to resolve a decades-long dispute over gay marriage and gay clergy.
>
> The proposal called "A Protocol of Reconciliation & Grace Through Separation," envisions an amicable separation in which conservative churches forming a new denomination would retain their assets. The new denomination also would receive $25 million.
>
> The proposal was signed in December by a 16-member panel, who worked with a mediator and began meeting in October. The panel was formed after it became clear the impasse over LGBTQ issues was irreconcilable. The next step could come at the church's General Conference in May."

CHAPTER NINETEEN

MEGACHURCHES

MEGACHURCHES ARE GREAT IF THEY ARE TEACHING AND living by God's Holy Word. Each of these larger churches minister to an average of two thousand members or more each week. Without doubt, some are God driven, while some are not.

The largest megachurches are in South Korea with one church claiming over 250,000 weekly attendees. The largest one in the USA is in Houston, and which is pastored by Joel Osteen and his wife. It is estimated that there are over two hundred such churches in Texas.

The Hartford Institute's database lists more than sixteen hundred and fifty (1650) such Protestant and Evangelical churches in the United States. According to their data, approximately fifty churches have weekly attendance ranging from 10,000 to 47,000.

It is estimated that the majority of US megachurches (over 70%) are in the southern Sunbelt with California, Texas, Florida and Georgia having the largest number. Many are in rapidly growing suburban areas of Los Angeles, Dallas, Atlanta, Houston, Orlando, Phoenix and Seattle.

According to some of the data obtained from Hartford Institute's research, the megachurches are made up as follows: 40% are non-denominational, 16% are Southern Baptists and the other 24% are among unspecified Baptists, Assembly of God, Christian, Calvary Chapel and United Methodists.

According to the Hartford Institute for Religion Research, the megachurch's theological orientation is 71%

Evangelical, 7% Moderate, 6% Missional, 5% Charismatic, 5% Pentecostal, 5% Seeker, 1% Fundamentalist, 0.5 Liberal and 1% other.

Many of these megachurches are *"multi-sited."* (They have multiple locations). It is today's method of delivering a message by satellite to other locations at multiple times and sites.

It is estimated that forty percent of these megachurches preach a gospel of prosperity which means that God wants us to be rich. Accordingly, *if you're not rich, it's your own fault.* I would interpret this to mean that you're not giving enough to the church. Therefore, God is not blessing you. A parishioner is expected to give more while the leadership becomes richer and richer. Prosperity-gospel preaching megachurches are well-oiled business enterprises with their collections being used to benefit those in leadership roles. Donations and tithes are used to buy homes, mansions, jet planes and fantastic trips.

✧ LAKEWOOD CHURCH/JOEL OSTEEN

Megachurches are accused of having a prosperity ministry which is very evident to those who are biblically oriented. A person listening intensely to Joel Osteen will know his motives after hearing his sermons and after reading his books.

Joel Osteen isn't alone in his prosperity endeavors. There are the likes of Joyce Meyer, Kenneth Copeland, T. D. Jakes, Robert Schuller, (deceased), Benny Hinn and numerous other. Is the public aware of a prosperity ministry? Apparently not, for the dollars roll into their coffers while personal jets are upgraded, and mansions are expanded.

The ministry of Rick Warren is under controversy. Who is Rick Warren and what are his beliefs? His present ministry is being questioned by many evangelicals.

The Joel Osteen megachurch in Houston has some fifty thousand plus members. It once had the word 'Baptist' in its name, but it was dropped so that it could become interdenominational in its outreach. The present pastors, Joel Osteen, a son of the founder, and his wife, Victoria, are copastors.

Imagine attending a church of such magnitude. Come early or you might not find a seat. It won't be like a smaller church where some members sit in the same pew Sunday after Sunday. Visualize visiting a smaller church one Sunday and after your finding a seat a member tells you that you're sitting in his or her seat. It won't happen to you in a megachurch, and it should not happen to you in a smaller congregation. Some members cling to certain routines.

God-driven megachurches are led by ministers preaching the words of repentance and redemption. These churches thrive on the Word of God and are aware of Jesus' saying,

> "I am the vine; you are the branches. If you remain
> in me and I in you, you will bear much fruit, apart
> from me you can do nothing" (John 15: 5).

These churches have very large staffs with many ministers. Yet, there are an untold number of unbelievers in the pew and on the membership rolls.

It is easier for members to become lost in a megachurch. Many of these members or attendees want only a little bit of religious activities each week. Perhaps, no more than one hour or two. They want to be left alone, to have no responsibilities and to have no tasks. A member can just remain a number on a church roll and can add the name of the church to his resume. Should a potential employer call for a verification, very little can be said about him. When he leaves the church: he won't be missed.

✢ ELEVATION CHURCH/STEVEN FURTICK

The following information for this mega-church was obtained from Wikipedia.

"Elevation church is a multi-site church and is pastured by Steven Furtick. The church has eighteen locations, nine in the Charlotte area, with additional locations in Raleigh, Greensboro, Winston Salem, Roanoke, (VA) Melbourne, (FL), and the Greater Toronto area. "Elevation Church was listed by Outreach magazine from 2007-2010 as one of the 100 fastest growing churches in the United States."

The church began as a church plant of The Baptist State Convention of North Carolina. As part of a church planting team, Steven Furtick and seven other families from Christ Covenant Church in Shelby, NC relocated to Matthews, NC, meeting in Providence High School.

The first Sunday worship service was held in February of 2008 with one hundred and twenty-one persons attending. The church in 2018 reported a regular attendance of about twenty-six thousand.

In 2008, Elevation Church gave out $40,000 to members in envelopes filled with $5, $20, even $1,000, and told them to spend it kindly on others.

Since 2010, Elevation Church has hosted a week-long outreach called "Love Week." During the church's 2010 Love Week, Elevation's members packed more than 10,000 sandwiches for the homeless, helped single mothers get their cars serviced, donated blood, cleaned up parks and streets, built a soccer field for local ministries and renovated buildings.

The church is not without its controversies. Elevation Church, and particularly its senior pastor, Steven Furtick, have caused controversy over the church's lack of financial transparency. and especially over Furtick's personal wealth and over questionable practices by the church.

In 2013, Furtick and his wife built a large house (8400 sq. ft. heated out of 16,000 sq. ft. total) on 19 acres of land in Waxhaw, NC, a suburb of Charlotte. The house and land are valued at just under $1.8 million.

Elevation Church has also been criticized over its practice of selecting volunteers who wish to be baptized during so-called "spontaneous baptism" services, which usually take place during normally scheduled weekend services. It is alleged that volunteers are asked to sit in prominent areas and instructed to respond immediately to Furtick's calls for volunteers to be baptized with the intent of inspiring genuine spontaneous baptisms.

CHAPTER TWENTY

TELE-EVANGELISTS

MY EXPERIENCE WITH SOME TELE-EVANGELISTS AND what is being preached through the airwaves, is not positive. Many messages are not about Jesus nor are they Bible-oriented. When the ministers do not lift-up the name of Jesus one should have some doubts about their authenticity.

✧ PRAISE THE LORD MINISTRY

James Orsen Bakker, a former Assemblies of God minister, (at one time married to Tammy Faye Bakker) founded the PTL (Praise the Lord) ministry in the Carolinas. The PTL Club opened in 1978 and closed in 1989.

The ministry operated as a talk show using many outstanding celebrities to boost its appeal. Donations of $1,000 were invited, and in return, a three day stay at its foundation were offered.

There were two things which brought Jim Bakker's ministry down: Sexual misconduct and illegal misuse of ministry funds. It is reported that $279,000 was paid out of ministry funds to an employed secretary, Jessica Hahn, to hush up an alleged sexual encounter she had with Mr. Bakker.

Jim Bakker initially received a sentence of forty-five years and a fine of $500,000 for his illegal activities, but in a later appeal of his conviction, it was reduced to eight years. He served less than five years of imprisonment, being release on parole in July 1994.

James Bakker, upon his release from prison, remarried and started *The Jim Bakker Show* in Blue Eye, MO which focuses on a nuclear apocalypse. It is reported to be flourishing.

Christians are forgetful of the past and some are very forgiving. It is said that one of Mr. Bakker's followers gave several million dollars to help him with his new project. The donor's generosity was attributed to his belief that Mr. Bakker had helped him in saving his marriage.

✣ JIMMY LEE SWAGGART

There is the saga of Jimmy Lee Swaggart, an American Pentecostal evangelist, whose television ministry began in 1971. His sexual encounters with prostitutes led the Assemblies of God to defrock him.

Mr. Swaggart had several sexual liaisons with prostitutes in New Orleans. He gave his well known, *"I Have Sinned"* sermon and pleaded for forgiveness. A few years later, he was caught with another prostitute. For a short period of time, he stepped down as the head of the Jimmy Swaggart Ministries.

He is now still pastoring a church in Louisiana and is doing Christian ministry. His efforts to start over again don't appear as successful as those of Mr. Bakker's.

There are others television evangelists which have their names on the tele-evangelists' *"Hall of Shame."* It's a very interesting list which would surprise some folks.

✣ JOYCE MEYER/ENJOYING EVERYDAY LIFE

She was born Pauline Joyce Hutchison on June 4, 1943. It is said that her father, a World War II veteran, after returning home from the service, sexually abused her.

Shortly after her senior year of high school, she married a part-time car salesman. The marriage lasted for five years, ending in 1966.

In 1967, she was married to Dave Meyer. Together, they raised four children who are now adults. Mr. Meyer's occupation is stated as an engineering draftsman.

Mrs. Meyer is known as being an author, writer, speaker, television evangelist, businessperson, teacher and preacher.

Her ministry is headquartered close to the St. Louis suburb of Fenton, MO. She makes her home outside of St. Louis, living in what is reported to be a 2 million-dollar home. Together, she and her husband have a 10 million-dollar jet and a boat worth more than one hundred thousand dollars. Her net worth is reported at 25 million dollars.

In 1985, Joyce Meyer, being very well known and popular, founded her own ministry, *"Life in the World."* Her book revenues add a lot to the size of her net worth. The Hachette Book Group paid just for contracting the right to print the list of independently publish books.

In 1993, Mrs. Meyer's husband, Dave, suggested that they start a television ministry.

In 1997, she hosted her own Christian television series, *Enjoying Everyday Life,* with an estimated 4.5 million or more viewers.

In 2005, she was ranked #17 in the list of the 25 Most Influential Evangelicals by Time magazine.

Joyce Meyer is criticized for her lavish lifestyle.

Television evangelists preaching a prosperity gospel shrug off their wealth as being a "gift from God" or a "blessing from God." It could also be described as *the less fortunate making the rich richer.*

✢ BILLY GRAHAM EVANGELISTIC ASSOCIATION

Billy Graham was a preacher called by God to preach the gospel of Jesus Christ to millions upon millions of people throughout the world. In his crusades, untold millions responded to his invitation to accept Jesus Christ as their Lord and Savior. He was accepted by Protestants and Catholics with his encouraging converts to unite with churches of their choice. Basically, it's unknown how many of these converts darkened the front door of a church after his crusades.

He counseled every president from Dwight D. Eisenhower to Barack Obama and was openly welcomed at and invited to the White House in Washington, DC.

Early in his ministry, Dr. Graham met with President Harry S. Truman at the White House. It is reported that President Truman made the claim that Dr. Graham was a publicity seeker. Probably this opinion by President Truman was a result of a later press conference held with Billy Graham and his team after their meeting.

The press wanted information from Dr. Graham about what had happened during the meeting with President Truman and was told that he had prayer with the President. The press asked to be shown how this had taken place in the White House. Billy Graham and his team knelt in prayer on the White House grounds to show what had occurred. It's believed that President Truman took issue with this display by Billy Graham and his team.

Early in Dr. Graham's ministry, he and his team adopted what some call the "Modesto Manifesto." Some would later call it the "Billy Graham Rule(s)." These rules addressed money, sexual immorality, relationship with churches, and publicity.

The rule on sexual immorality was that "the team would avoid any situation that would even have the appearance of compromise or suspicion." From that point on, Dr. Graham did not travel, meet, or eat alone with a woman other than his wife. (Sinclair Lewis' fictional book in 1926, *Elmer Gantry* had depicted evangelists in a dismal light, and there were other Elmer Gantry type evangelists during the time of Dr. Graham's ministry.)

He noted that on one occasion during one of his Little Rock crusades, he was asked by Mrs. Hillary Clinton to have a private lunch meeting with her. "I would be delighted to," I replied. "but I don't have private luncheons with beautiful ladies."

"We could sit in the middle of the dining room at the Capital Hotel where everybody would be able to see us," she said, "and still have a private conversation." (Billy Graham's autobiography, page 651, "*Just as I Am*") And, according to Dr. Graham: "We did."

From the jacket of his book *Just as I Am,* the following is noted about Dr. Graham's ministry to the masses:

> "Hailed as the world's preacher, his calling as an Evangelist has taken him to every nation, from Europe to Asia, from major capitals to the most remote outposts. His Crusades have spanned fifty years…"

> "A pioneer in social issues (he refused to preach to segregated audiences in the South), he has led by his extraordinary example of integrity."

Dr. Graham's son, Franklin, now heads up the Billy Graham Evangelistic Association.

✢ PREYING ON THE NEEDY

My mother, who is now deceased, sent donations to a self-proclaimed radio minister who sent prayer cloths and other items which were *"anointed by him and the Lord"* to do wonders for her infirmities. He was quite demanding when the donations ceased.

Many tele-evangelists flood the air waves with requests for funds to support their ministries. They try any appeal to receive funds to further what they claim is the Lord's work but used instead by some for their own desired lifestyles.

Mr. Bakker made an appeal for three million plus dollars to send across the water for the message of Jesus to be preached. When received, the funds remained at home.

Oral Roberts made his well-known appeal for eight million dollars. He received his funds which enabled him to come down from his tower and to build a Christian hospital in Tulsa.

Tele-evangelists reach large audiences, not only in America, but overseas. Their approach for money is successful. Multitudes believe that these tele-evangelists are doing the Lord's work and that their donations will reach others with the gospel message. The Bible is not known well and studied by many of these listeners. Therefore, there isn't any way for them to know what's truth or fiction.

There isn't a way for a novice to know good wine from bad wine. There isn't a way for an unbeliever or one who hasn't been born again to know anything in the spiritual realm.

✢ ABOUT TITHING

A favorite biblical passage used by television evangelists is found in the Old Testament.

> Bring the whole tithe into the storehouse, that there
> may be food in my house. Test me in this, says the
> Lord Almighty, and see if I will not throw open the
> floodgates of heaven and pour out so much blessing
> that there will not be room enough to store it (Mal.
> 3: 10).

The Israelites (Jews) had to take care of the Levites priestly
ministry. They brought their sacrifices to the altar and parts
of it were given to the needy and those serving in places of
worship. The intent wasn't to allow those serving the Lord to
have mansions, jets, tailored suits, and faster automobiles, but
to sustain their needs.

Reading the passage from Malachi further, here is what
the blessing is to be:

> I will prevent pests from devouring your crops
> and the vines in your fields will not stop your fruit
> before it is ripe, says the Lord Almighty. Then all
> the nations will call you blessed, for yours will be
> a delightful land, says the Lord Almighty (Mal. 3:
> 11-12).

It is obvious from God's Word that the Lord God expects
a tenth of our income. Many Christians, born again believers,
don't tithe a tenth of their income. Some will tithe on their net
income but not on the gross. Some won't tithe because they
say it's not in the New Testament.

✣ WHAT SOME SAY ABOUT TITHING

I was seated next to a lady in church one Sunday. She
leaned over to me and asked, *"Where in the Bible does it say that
we are to tithe?"* Hastily, I wrote down a few verses for her from

the Old Testament. After reading my response, she handed me her response: *"Where in the New Testament?"*

Immediately, I knew where she was coming from. We are to believe what is written in the OT as well as what is written in the NT. The Bible is not a pick and choose book. This is true for any matter, whether it involves money, loving another, divorce, adultery, sex, homosexuality, taking care of the poor, widows, the needy, etc. The tithe is not meant to make a television or radio evangelist wealthier.

The Apostle Paul had this to say about his ministry:

> I have not coveted anyone's silver or gold or clothing. You yourselves know that these hands of mine have supplied my own needs and the needs of my companions. In everything I did, I showed you that by this kind of hard work we must help the weak, remembering the words the Lord Jesus himself said: 'it is more blessed to give than to receive' (Acts 20: 33-35).

It is interesting that these words of Paul, "remembering the words the Lord Jesus himself said: 'it is more blessed to give than to receive,'" isn't written elsewhere in the New Testament. Some doubters will question this and ask, "Since the apostle didn't sit under the teaching of Jesus, where did Paul hear this?" Jesus may have included these words in his meeting with Paul at his conversion, or it may have been told to him by one of the apostles.

Recall from the Gospel according to Saint John:

> Jesus did many other things as well, if every one of them were written down, I suppose that even the whole world would not have room for the books that would be written (John 21: 25).

Are some television evangelists helping to spread the gospel to people across the globe? Yes! All TV evangelists are not out for the money. Some are for real, while some are not. Some are Christians and they belong to Christ Jesus. Some are an Elmer Gantry of this day and their intent is to fill their own coffers.

Here is what Jesus had to say:

> "Teacher," said John, "we saw someone driving out demons in your name and we told him to stop, because he was not one of us." "Do not stop him," Jesus said. "For no one who does a miracle in my name can in the next moment said anything bad about me, for whoever is not against us is for us. Truly I tell you, anyone who gives you a cup of water in my name because you belong to the Messiah will certainly not lose their reward" (Mark 9: 38-41).

The mention of God's Word is often used by those who are not true Christians.

God will permit television evangelists to preach their prosperity message and to use the funds to support their lavish lifestyles. The use of the Name of Jesus in their messages for wealth may reach into the hearts of some viewers to quicken their thirst for a Redeemer.

The Apostle Paul had this to say about those who preach Christ out of selfish ambition:

> But what does it matter? The important, thing is that in every way, whether from false motives or true, Christ is preached. And because of this I rejoice (Phil. 1:18a).

CHAPTER TWENTY-ONE

MODERN DAY CHURCHES AND MINISTERS

✢ AT THE SEMINARY/INSTITUTIONS OF LEARNING

COURSES CAN BE TAUGHT ON SPIRITUALITY AT ANY institution. However, spirituality comes only from God.

In the early 1960s, outside the chapel at the New Orleans Baptist Theological Seminary, a small group of seminary students was huddled. A member of the group remarked, *"I wish that I were wealthy and when I get called to a church, I could preach the way that God wants me to preach."*

This statement has remained with me for almost sixty years. It was a meaningful remark by a student as to whether to preach the messages of God or the messages dictated by church members. It was a statement by a student of theology which could have been said by others in the group and in other institutions of learning as well. The expression was very thought provoking.

One student within this group was already making his mark by being the associate pastor of a very large church, and who had dreams of evangelistic meetings as large as those of Dr. Billy Graham. But, for that matter, don't we all have our own wishes and desires?

Being a preacher myself, I know that ministers know very early what type of sermons their congregations want to hear. True preachers know what they need to preach, but some don't preach it. Which comes first, the chicken or the egg? The reason for God's *calling* is to proclaim the messages which God will give. These messages come from God to his servants through the Holy Spirit.

A spiritually minded person can distinguish a God called person from a vocational called minister. A God called minister will preach what God has "called" him to do. God will put into his mouth the words which he wants preached. A vocationally called person enters the ministry only as an occupation or a career. He is there for the paycheck.

Jesus says,

> "I am the good shepherd. "The good shepherd lays down his life for the sheep. The hired hand is not the shepherd and does not own the sheep. So when he sees the wolf coming, he abandons the sheep and runs away. Then the wolf attacks the flock and scatters it. The man runs away because he is a hired hand and cares nothing for the sheep" (John 10: 11-13).

The God called minister is the shepherd. The vocationally call minister is a hireling.

What is the difference between some preachers and other preachers? Politicians promise most anything to their constituents, and more often than not, never try. Preachers might not make promises to their people, but some do become political in their ministry.

Whether one is God called or vocationally called, most ministers will claim that they are God called. Messages being preached from pulpits across America today is indicative that many ministers of churches are not led by the Spirit of God.

✢ WISHES OR DESIRES

W.I. Thomas (1863-1947), an American sociologist, identified four desires of people: the wish for new experiences; the wish for security; the wish for response; and the wish for recognition. His teaching is that these four wishes or desires are present in all of us, but one of them becomes our major desire.

In many of my relationship with acquaintances, I would guess that the desire for security saturates most people lives more than any other desire. Should I guess about the other three wishes as to their importance: I believe that the desire for response takes second place, then recognition, and lastly, new experiences.

My fellow seminarian was expressing a desire for security when he remarked that you had to preach what the people in churches wanted to hear. His desire for security was his motivating force and was prevalent to him. By not knowing too much about his previous experience within a church, his statement could have been based upon what he had been told or had already witnessed. Undoubtedly, he was expressing a desire to preach what the Lord would want him to preach. Recognition was probably the desire of the one who was an associate at a large church and his becoming an evangelist with large crowds at his crusades.

✢ APOSTLE PAUL'S DESIRE FOR MINISTERS

The apostle Paul expressed these words to Timothy, his fellow worker in the faith:

> For the time will come when people will not put up with sound doctrine. Instead, to suit their own desires, they will gather around them a great number of teachers to say what their itching ears

want to hear. They will turn their ears away from
the truth and turn aside to myths" (2 Tim. 4: 3-4).

Paul's desire for his fellow workers was to stay in the faith
and to preach the Word.

There are ministers today who are called by God to
preach the message of the gospel and to make disciples,
baptizing them in the name of the Father, Son and the Holy
Spirit. There are others who enter the profession by their own
choosing. It becomes a professional career and is not a calling
by the Lord.

The calling of God of ministers to preach his truths is not
an easy one. One's task isn't to adhere to the wishes of the
people to whom he is called to serve. Moses is a good example.
God placed a heavy burden on his shoulders. A burden much
heavier than the one which Moses had experienced prior
to his calling. God does the calling and not people. He also
does the choosing. The issue of whether a minister is God-
called or vocationally called can't be stressed enough. There
is a difference when genuine items are being sold and when
imitations are offered. So, it is with ministers.

✢ MINISTERS WITH SOUPY AND SYRUPY INGREDIENTS

There are some ministers who are not called by God.
Some of them know very little about the Bible. To them the
Bible might be only a book of history, poetry, or just a book
with many stories about mankind.

There are ministers throughout the world serving churches
who have never tasted the blood of the Lord Jesus. They are
interested in making a living and to have a voice in the affairs
of their community and throughout their regions. While there

are men of the cloth who are sincere in their approach to reach others for Christ.

Putting the word "Reverend" before a name, doesn't make a person worthy of reverence and respect.

Elmer Gantry was a satirical novel written and published by Sinclair Lewis in the 1920's which caused a stir in America. Some, even newspapers, called for the book to be banned. Later, it would be made into a movie with Burt Lancaster playing the leading role. Today, it wouldn't cause a call for banishment by the public, since many Gantry types are past, present and future.

Some of today's preachers are of the Elmer Gantry types. Many churchgoers are taken in by those who are charismatic, loving their sermons whether gospel or not.

In later chapters, I will discuss some of the preachers which I have been acquainted with in my journey within churches here in America.

CHAPTER TWENTY-TWO

SOUPY INGREDIENTS WITHIN CHURCHES

TODAY'S CHURCHES ARE INFILTRATED WITH PEOPLE WHO have never repented of their sins and have never had a personal relationship with Jesus Christ. Churches have always been infiltrated by non-believers since biblical times. Saint Peter and Saint Paul had their problems with heretics who had infiltrated churches with their false doctrines. The teaching of these infiltrators was leading people away from the truth by teaching that Jesus Christ was not totally human and not totally God.

The trends in today's churches are many. These movements are spreading like wildfire and some are more covert and difficult to detect.

Most churchgoers are illiterates with respect to the Bible. So little is known about the Bible and its teachings that many are led to believe that any and every inventive doctrine by man is the truth.

Church rolls consist of many types of parishioners. There are the liberal, traditional, and conservative thinkers and some who are not thinkers at all.

✝ THE INFILTRATION

Churches are filled with many types of people each with a different personality. Some will be more mature than others, and some will be babes in Christ. Only one ingredient is important in the makeup of a church: born again believers. However, churches are made up of two types of ingredients: believers and unbelievers. And, from experience and the opinions of many scholars and students of the Bible, unbelievers are in the majority. That statement will be shocking to some.

Straight from the mouth of Jesus comes even a bolder statement:

> "For many are invited, but few are chosen" (Matt. 22:14).

This could be strengthened with other passages from God's Holy Word. However, it's not necessary. Many churchgoing folks aren't true representatives of the Christian faith. But, because of their Christian representation, unbelievers outside the walls of the church believe that churchgoing folks are relics of the Christian faith. Jesus, upon his return, will be the one separating the sheep from the goats. Of course, the sheep are disciples of Christ, and the goats: people belonging to the devil.

> "When the Son of Man comes in his glory, and all the angels with him, he will sit on his glorious throne. All the nations will be gathered before him, and he will separate the people one from another as a shepherd separates the sheep from the goats. He will put the sheep on his right and goats on his left" (Matt. 25: 31-33).

The Head of the church is Jesus. The church is His Bride. Members of some churches replace Jesus with their desires and thirst for recognition. People like to be seen and heard.

Unbelievers are unable to be biblically and spiritually led but will dictate their own policies within the confines of the church. Members of any church who have not had a personal relationship with the Lord Jesus will not have the Holy Spirit living inside of them. The Holy Spirit comes only to reside within believers. There isn't any possible way that an unbeliever can understand spiritual values.

> The person without the Spirit does not accept the things that come from the Spirit of God but considers them foolishness and cannot understand them because they are discerned only through the Spirit. The person with the Spirit makes judgments about all things, but such a person is not subject to merely human judgments (1 Cor. 2: 14-15).

The word *'Spirit'* in the above passage is capitalized four times because only believers have the *'Spirit"* of God living within them. Unbelievers have only the *'spirit'* of man within.

Some might ask, how did such a situation develop within the doors of our churches? Infiltrating was present on the day of Pentecost. Judas Iscariot was an infiltrator within the group of the twelve but wasn't the first infiltrator in the Christian church. Judas' physical life ended before the cross. Infiltrating will always remain. A matter had arisen within the church of Galatia about baptism. Paul had this to say:

> This matter arose because some false believers had infiltrated our ranks to spy on the freedom we have in Christ Jesus and to make us slaves. We did not give in to them for a moment, so that the truth of the gospel might be preserved for you (Gal. 2: 4-5).

How many infiltrators or unbelievers are on the rolls of churches? It's impossible to know. They appear in sheep's clothing but are living like ravaging wolves.

Years ago, a preacher friend of mine and I discussed this question: How many goats are there in churches? We could only speculate about the number. Large crowds sought Jesus during his three and one-half years of ministry. Were they looking only for the miracles which He was performing? Many called Him "Lord," but refused to do the things which He asked of them. The New Testament Church started with one hundred twenty (120) individuals who were gathered in a room awaiting the Promise of the Father on the day of Pentecost. Undoubtedly, they were not infiltrated at that time.

CHAPTER TWENTY-THREE

MY CALLING

✚ MY LIFE AS A MINISTER

IT WOULD BE UNETHICAL OF ME WHILE WRITING THIS book, if I didn't write about my career as a minister. It is true that I am critical about those who claim to speak for God. I will write about my several experiences and my observations about ministers.

When I was twenty-six years of age, God saved me while flat-on-my-back in my bedroom at home. My physician had instructed me to stay bedridden for at least six weeks to overcome the rheumatic fever which I was experiencing.

It was then-all alone with God-I was not only saved, but was called as a minister to serve him. I made a promise to God that when this illness was behind me, I would go to the Baptist church up-the-road and make my acknowledgement of Him before others. This I did. But what I didn't do, was announce my calling as a minister.

Once over my sickness, I returned to the same old routine of making a living. There remained no peace and joy within my soul which should have been mine after being saved. It was over a year later, thinking that my unhappiness was in my employment, I left my job, sold my home, and moved to Florida with my family.

Arriving in Florida, finding another vocation, and with the purchase of another house, I found the emptiness returned. There was still the lack of peace. Six months later, my family and I packed up our belongings and headed to New Orleans for me to attend a Baptist Seminary as a theology student.

Leaving the seminary almost three years later with a degree in theology, we returned to Orlando seeking a church or wherever the Lord God was willing to lead me.

✤ THE CALLING OF MINISTERS WITHIN SOME DENOMINATIONS

Things were done somewhat differently in those days. It was unthinkable or unethical for a Baptist minister to send a resume to a church which was absent a preacher. The method used at that time was for an acquaintance, a friend, a family member, a seminary or someone in the church which one was attending, to put one's name before a church which was seeking a minister.

Churches without preachers had pulpit committees which would visit other Baptist churches to hear ministers who already had pulpits. It was a tough and long road for those of us who were inexperienced in the ministry.

My first pastorate came through the recommendation of the pastor of the First Baptist Church in Winter Garden, FL. Previously, he had given my name to a close-by church, with a very wealthy membership, where I had spent one Sunday preaching trial sermons. With my not getting a calling from this church, this same pastor recommended me to the First Baptist Church, in Lake Mary, FL. They issued a call after having me do trial sermons. My ordination to the ministry was performed at Pine Hill Baptist Church in Orlando.

I must confess, my calling to the ministry wasn't meant for a long-term relationship in any church. I would preach to the same group of people Sunday after Sunday with very little, if any, results. Frankly, that is what I have been called to do-to serve congregational needs and to reach the lost. But, in some churches, reaching the lost isn't prevalent. And, to preach to the same faces week after week wasn't what I believed that the Lord God had called me to do. My ministry was to be an evangelistic one.

So, after four months at Lake Mary, I gave my resignation notice to the deacons and the membership. I regret doing that, but two-services on Sunday and one on Wednesday nights with the same group of people wasn't my calling.

While at the seminary in New Orleans, I had heard about virgin territory in the northwestern part of the United States. I returned to my hometown Atlanta and worked for two or three months painting a relative's house to gain funds for my trip to Seattle.

In the meantime, I wrote to the Southern Baptist Home Mission Broad to inquire about any possible openings in the Washington state area. I heard nothing from them until I was later established in Tacoma and pastoring a church. The letter advised me that there was nothing available in the Northwest.

✢ A TRIP OF FAITH

My wife, my son, and I left Atlanta pulling a U-Haul trailer for the missionary and pastoring opportunities in the beautiful state of Washington. Arriving in Seattle, I never went a Sunday without preaching. God opened doors and put me in contact with Christians who were eager to help.

A minister, who was a dermatologist, filled the pulpit of a Baptist church in Seattle, and was preaching without any renumeration. He invited me to preach some of the services. Doors were being opened.

A Southern Baptist Associational missionary in Seattle was very helpful. He had preached at a Baptist church in Tacoma on a previous Sunday and had been invited back to preach the next Sunday. Not wanting to go back, he asked me if I would go in his place.

There was a reason for his not wanting to go back. "That church is split down the middle," he exclaimed. They are almost at the stage of physical fighting among themselves. "I'm not asking you to go down there in the hope of them calling you to pastor. They are not ready for a minister until they can get themselves together."

I went to Tacoma in his place that Sunday and two weeks later was extended a call to become their pastor. In a few months, the split was repaired as the people came together. I was on the church field for one year when electing to finish my college education at California Baptist University (then a college) in Riverside.

✢ LIFE IN RIVERSIDE

My family and I joined a Baptist Church in Riverside where many of the professors from the college attended. I was lacking two years of credits in getting my Bachelor of Arts degree. I should have finished my college before attending the seminary, but I was in a hurry to get into the preaching of God's Word.

It was soon after arriving in Riverside that a Baptist church, where my family and I were attending, called me as its associate pastor. It was there that I became the associate to a very prayerful and dedicated pastor. He was a true man of God who was instrumental in starting the church which he was now serving. Looking back, I would say that it was the most spiritual church which I have ever attended or been a part of. The church was large and growing almost every Sunday.

One thing which I learned from Pastor Pope was that church didn't just happen within the walls of a building, but also in neighborhoods where the people were. When visitors attended the services on Sunday mornings, before the sun set that night, he and I had knocked on their door. Pastor Pope was a great man of prayer and action.

After graduation from college, I went back to Washington seeking another pastorate, but to no avail. There were no church openings. The decision was soon made to return to Atlanta to be near family members and to seek a pastorate there.

God wasn't through with me yet.

I will conclude for now my brief history as a minister up to this point and will pick it up again in the next chapter. Getting away from the will of God is one of the reasons for **THE KILLING OF THE CHRISTIAN CHURCH IN AMERICA.**

CHAPTER TWENTY-FOUR

POLITICS WITHIN THE CHURCH

BACK HOME IN ATLANTA, THE FOOTWORK BEGAN OF making contacts with ministers within local ministerial associations as well as members within the local church where my family and I would be attending. It soon became an exhausting process.

A fair number of local ministers in the ministerial association in and around Atlanta were graduates of the Southern Baptist Seminary in Louisville, an institution noted for looking out for its own. Up until this point, I was unfamiliar with the smoking habits of those standing in the pulpit. Without doubt, it was an acceptable habit within this group. Over the years, especially back then, I breathed in a lot of second-hand smoke getting to the front door of a church.

✢ MY MOTHER'S PASTORS

My mother was a devoted member of a local Baptist church in her neighborhood. She loved the Lord and was a faithful attendee of His church. Before my conversion, she would have my family and me over for dinner on many occasions. Of course, unexpectantly, her pastor would show up at some of these and would witness to me about the Lord Jesus. Upon my conversion some years later, I was well acquainted with the Roman Road to salvation and many other passages.

One of her ministers who visited with me while at her home was later accused and proven to be gay. He would later take his life. It didn't shake her faith, since she never believed that which was said about him was true.

✢ THE PLACING OF MY NAME BEFORE A CHURCH

I had a first cousin who was attending a Baptist church some forty or fifty miles away from Atlanta which was without a pastor. He approached the pulpit committee about me, and the committee added my name to their list of candidates. They asked me to preach a trial sermon in another church. This was a custom for potentials to be heard away from the church which was in need of a pastor.

Arrangements were made with my mother's pastor to permit me to use his pulpit at a Sunday night's service. The church where I was going to preach my trial sermon was one of these "going out of business" churches. Whites in the neighborhood were moving to the suburbs and blacks were moving in. It would be just a matter of time before its closing.

The pulpit committee came, the committee heard, but there was no call. After a couple of weeks, I asked my cousin about my status. "You haven't heard because the pastor where you preached, told the pulpit committee that he would be interested." He had a "Dr." before his name, was much more experienced, and a much better resume.

✢ MINISTRY VERSES THE BUSINESS WORLD

I had to move on: my family needed shelter, clothes and food. So, I went back into the world of work. I thought perhaps God had only called me for a short-term ministry, and I had already fulfilled His purpose for my calling. I searched the

Scriptures to see if I could find evidence of that being the situation. Not certain about whether my calling had ended, I was truthful in every job interview that I was a preacher, and if I received a calling, I wouldn't remain.

The Atlanta Public Schools had a need for a counselor, and the slot was temporarily funded year-to-year. Therefore, they had no concern for my being subject to leave.

Less than a year later, I was taken out of counseling and moved to an administrative position in vocational education. For the next five to six years, increased salaries and promotions came my way.

Meanwhile, my family and I were attending a Baptist church in Decatur, where the congregation was becoming increasingly unhappy with the pastor. He was encouraged to take some time off while some within the membership wanted to get their facts and figures together before dismissing him. I was invited to fill the pulpit but refused their invitation. I felt a loyalty to one of my own. If our preacher was a God-called man, it was up to the Lord to remove him.

Another invitation and call came from another church, but I had debt obligations from the purchase of property and a house stood in the way. Yet, I was still doing some preaching on a few occasions.

✢ Divorce, Remarriage and Consequences

Afterwards, a catastrophic happening took place in my life. I left my wife of some twenty-four years. She was a devoted, caring and churchgoing woman. We were divorced a few months later. "What a wretched man I am! Who will rescue me from this body that is subject to death" (Rom. 7:24)?

I remarried and for the next twenty-two years, I lived to regret that mistake. Basically, I left the ministry for those twenty-two years, except for my serving as an associate pastor in a United Methodist Church in Alabama.

The pastor at the church where my Methodist wife and I were attending, approached me about coming aboard as his assistant on a part-time basis. I had not pursued it or was I interested. How could I stand in the pulpit and preach to others about living Christian lives when I had violated my marital vows and had divorced my first wife of twenty-four years?

"The people have such a respect for you," Pastor Chandler insisted. "Besides, I need help."

Pastor Chandler was a godly and loving man who knew his time here on earth was limited because of a bone condition. The people were sympathetic of his condition and loved him as much as he loved them. In my analysis, he was a true man of the cloth. Marcus Chandler took only fifteen minutes in the pulpit to get God's message to the people. There were no redundancies in his messages - only the facts.

I served with him for a period-of-time before moving out of state to take a job offer with a couple of young entrepreneurs in North Carolina.

After moving to North Carolina, I divorced my second wife due to her unfaithfulness. After approximately four years of bachelorhood, I married my third wife, and we have been together for twenty-three years. We are now churchgoing members in a Baptist church.

I have served as an interim minister at a couple of Baptist churches since moving to North Carolina and have been involved in jail and prison ministries and led several Bible studies. I am at peace with the Lord God.

✣ YOU BE THE JUDGE

So, what kind of preacher or person am I? Would you care to sit under my preaching and allow me to tell you how to be a faithful mate and how to raise your children. People who are Christians and love the Lord make mistakes. I have found that He doesn't give up on them. He finds ways in which he can use them.

Pastor Charles Stanley of First Baptist Church in Atlanta separated from his wife of forty-four years in 1992, and she filed for divorce in 1993 while he was serving as the senior pastor. Much isn't known about the details or the reasons for their divorce or whether it was later changed to a legal separation. That should not be an issue.

Dr. Stanley is an outstanding man of the cloth. He has incredulous credentials. And the mega church which he is pastoring, appears to be thriving. I have personally heard him on television from time to time. He is known and respected for preaching the Word of God. He did the right thing by staying in the ministry after his divorce or separation. But in my case, I am sure that my reasons and circumstances of staying out of the ministry were different.

CHAPTER TWENTY-FIVE

DEFINING TITLES

STATUS CONSCIOUS INDIVIDUALS LOVE TITLES. WHILE working in the business world, I became aware of how some people in the workforce love a title. Give a person a title and you can forget having to give a pay increase for a while. A job holder in the secular world may become a specialist, an expert, or an engineer. For example, upon entering a chain restaurant one evening which specializing in steaks, a waitress announced her name and identified herself as being my steak-logistic for the evening meal.

✢ A FEW DEFINITIONS

PREACHER: One who preaches. One who publicly proclaims the gospel as an occupation.

PASTOR: A Christian minister having spiritual charge over a congregation or parish. A shepherd.

MINISTER: One authorized to perform religious functions in a church, especially a protestant church. Preachers, pastors, ministers and reverends perform the same functions. To attend to the needs and wants of others. To perform the functions of a member of the clergy.

REVEREND: One worthy of reverence. Used as a title for a cleric.

FATHER: A priest or clergyman in the Roman Catholic, Anglican, or Eastern Orthodox churches. Used as a title.

PRIEST: 1. A member of the second grade of clergy ranking below a bishop but over a deacon and having authority to pronounce absolution and administer all sacraments save that of ordination in the Roman Catholic, Eastern Orthodox, Anglican, Armenian, and separated Catholic hierarchies. 2. One whose role is considered comparable to that of a priest.

RABBI: 1. An ordained spiritual leader of a Jewish congregation. 2. One authorized to interpret Jewish law.

These definitions were adapted from Webster's International New College Dictionary, Houghton Mifflin Company, Boston – New York, 1995.

Individuals using these titles should, when preforming functions within a church, be ordained.

No attempt on my part has been made to research The U. S. Labor Department manual, *The Dictionary of Occupational Titles,* which describes in detail the functions of every existing, imaginable job title. Often, after each description, these words are added, "and any other duties as required."

Some denominational churches, which are autonomous, seek out and employ their ministers. Some denominations with appointed bishops, cardinals and other church leaders, assign ministers or priests to churches within their territorial authority. These assignments may be short or long term. In some denominations, the leadership reads and edits the sermons before being preached by their appointees, and they will use established formats.

Autonomous led churches will seek some or most of the following attributes or characteristics in a minister, preacher, pastor, reverend or shepherd. Some of these features are found in those who are in the clergy, but not all.

EXPERIENCED
THEOLOGICAL
DOCTINALLY SOUND
ORATORICAL
CHARISMATIC
SPIRITUAL MINDED
EVANGELISTIC
SMYPATHETIC
DYNAMIC
CIVIC MINDED
PERSONABLE
OFFICIATE AT WEDDINGS AND FUNERALS
CONVERSATIONAL
EDUCATED
LOVING
KIND
DEDICATED
COMPASSINATE

Whether the church has a large membership or small-in-number, a church will seek many of these qualifications in a person who fills their pulpit.

To these attributes and characteristics, I will add these requirements:

A MAN WHO TOTALLY BELIEVES IN WHAT HE IS PREACHING

A MAN WHO BELIEVES THE BIBLE IS RELEVANT FOR TODAY'S SOCIETY.

A MAN WHO BELIEVES THAT THE WORDS WHICH HE IS PREACHING ARE COMING DIRECTLY FROM GOD

A MAN WHO PREACHES TO PLEASE GOD
AND NOT THE PARISHIONERS

A MAN WHO BELIEVES THAT HE IS
UNDER THE INSPIRITION OF THE HOLY
SPIRIT

A MAN WHO PRACTICES WHAT HE
PREACHES

A MAN WHO LOVES EACH AND EVERY
ONE OF THOSE TO WHOM HE PREACHES

Some churches will want their minister to preach two or three times each week, especially those churches which have an early service and a traditional one.

Are their churches today who would invite, accept and permit a minister to be their leader if he were weak, trembling, fearful, lacking eloquence and without human wisdom in his messages?

During the New Testament era the church at Corinth had such a person as their leader.

> When I came to you, I did not come with eloquence or human wisdom as I proclaimed to you the testimony about God. For I resolved to know nothing while I was with you except Jesus Christ and him crucified. I came to you in weakness with great fear and trembling. My message and my preaching were not with wise and persuasive words, but with a demonstration of the Spirit's power, so that your faith might not rest on human wisdom, but on God's power (1 Cor. 2: 1b-5).

The "I" in this passage was Paul, the apostle to the gentiles. I do not believe Paul was bad. He was merely not highly trained in Greek rhetoric. The fear and trembling were in reference to humility before God.

Why, in this book, do I devote so much to writing about ministers, preachers, pastors, reverends, priests, fathers, teachers and church leaders? The reason is a simple one: in today's world, the majority of "these men of the cloth" are vocationally called and not spiritually led. They have become mere employees filling a role meant only for the God called.

The Old Testament writings are filled with numerous pages of false prophets doing the same for wages. They proclaim peace when there is no peace.

> They dress the wounds of my people as though it were not serious. 'Peace, peace,' they say, when there is no peace (Jer. 6:14).

> "Because they lead my people astray, saying "Peace," when there is no peace, and because, when a flimsy wall is built, they cover it with whitewash" (Ezekiel 13:10).

The number one cause for **THE KILLING OF THE CHRISTIAN CHURCH IN AMERICA**, are pulpiteers who proclaim that they are called and speaking for God. Churches in every denomination appoint ministers who are vocationally called, gays, lesbians, and atheists. Some denominations appoint women to be their shepherd, when there isn't a biblical basis.

The blind is leading the blind. Jesus told them this parable: "Can the blind lead the blind? Will they not both fall into a pit?" (Luke 6:39).

Am I being judgmental of others? Perhaps, I am. I prefer to call my judging of others merely a critiquing, and not a criticism. There is such a decline and decay within the church. God knows the answer to this question.

Ministers are responsible for the large number of unsaved on their church roles. When individuals come forward for church membership, they are usually asked questions which require only a *"yes."* For example, when a person comes forward for baptism or church membership and the minister asks: Do you come on your profession of faith in Jesus Christ?" Answer, "yes." "Do you believe that Jesus died for your sins?" Answer, "yes." "Do you believe that God raised Jesus from the dead?" Answer, "yes." The confessors are then turned loose to paddle their own canoes and to enter the lake alone. Some churches require "orientation classes," but one's relationship to Jesus is not often discussed.

A question about repentance is seldom or never asked by the minister. Have you had a personal experience with the Lord Jesus? Do you believe that the blood of Jesus has cleansed you of your sins? Such questions might never be asked.

✢ SEARS, ROEBUCK & COMPANY

Great institutions come and go. Sears, Roebuck & Company, an American retail giant, was gigantic in marketing its wares in bygone years. The Sears, Roebuck & Company's catalog reached into millions of homes and was put-to-use in outhouses in rural areas where toilet paper was not available. Even houses could be purchased from its catalog.

Mr. Sears built a nine-story, a city within a city, merchandise building on a forty-acre tract in Chicago in 1905-1906 which was the tallest building in Chicago at that time. Its towers reached the height of a fourteen-story building. In the 1990s, the nine-story warehouse was demolished. Now, some twenty to thirty years later, Sears, Roebuck & Company is no longer a competitor in the retail market and is slowly disappearing into the sunset. And, so is the Christian church.

Churches across America try different programs and methods in their pursuit of enlarging their membership rolls. These rolls are padded with members whose names appear on the rolls of other churches as well. Churches have the names of members on their rolls who are members of another church or denomination. Those who have come by statement and not by letter. In Christian stats, many members are counted more than once. Church rolls contain members which have not been heard from in years and who are impossible to locate.

Americans live in a mobile society. Those members who go from one denomination to another by statement or letter might not be acceptable at another church. Those who come from denominations where sprinkling is the method of baptizing, are required to be immersed. Churches do refuse to go through their rolls and remove names. It is believed that there are millions of members being carried on church rolls who are being double counted in surveys.

Slowly, year by year, churches and their buildings will disappear from the scene. The continued decline of the church is evident. Churches will disappear, but not the Christianity in those who are God's children.

CHAPTER TWENTY-SIX

BEING JUDGMENTAL OF PREACHERS

✧ PLANTING SEEDS

HERE ARE SOME WORDS GIVEN TO YOUNG TIMOTHY BY the Apostle Paul:

> Preach the word; be prepared in season and out of season; correct, rebuke and encourage - with great patience and careful instruction (2 Tim. 4:2).

Paul, addressing the church at Corinth, had this to write:

> "I planted the seed, Apollos watered it, but God has been making it grow. So neither the one who plants nor the one who waters, is anything, but only God, who makes things grow" (1 Cor. 3: 6-7).

The problem today is that good seeds of the gospel are not being planted or watered by true disciples of Christ. The watering which is being done benefits only the weeds. More and more who profess to be Christians are choking out any good done by true parishioners.

One of the reasons for **THE KILLING OF THE CHRISTIAN CHURCH IN AMERICA** is due to the Word of God not being preached. The old-time ministers are fading into the sunset, and whether God will bring future revivals and raise up preachers of his choosing isn't known.

God could be through with professed Christianity in America. He is a long-suffering, patient God. He gave up on the disobedient Israelites and allowed them to spend years in captivity. The Old Testament reveals that the patience of God with his people, the Israelites, finally came to an end.

Throughout America, people have started churches to benefit themselves. They didn't like what was happening in their church, so they formed churches to conform to their beliefs and desires. Splits have been a factor in initiating the starting-up of multiple churches. Many of these splits are preacher-bred.

✛ HOMILETICS

Homiletics, or the teaching or the art of the formulation of sermons and preaching, was taught at the seminary which I attended. It was a required course for theology students. Being taught how to develop a sermon or as some might say *"a homily,"* is very important for the novice. Only God the Father can give to one the words and wisdom. God says this to those he calls:

> Then the Lord reached out his hand and touched my mouth and said to me, "I have put my words in your mouth" (Jer. 1: 9).

Many pulpiteers develop three-or-four-point sermons. I have done the same. Taking these pointers together with a few verses of scripture, a homily is delivered. Some preachers elaborate on three or four points and will often depart into the sunset without asking God to fill in the words.

I have heard and experienced many of these three-or-four-point sermons. So have the multitudes. This is what parishioners are familiar with and no doubt want to hear. These three or four pointer sermons are easier to write down and remember. Masses will call this preaching, and for some, it is. "Oh, wasn't that a wonderful sermon?" Or, "I enjoyed your message."

These sermons often come after hours spent researching commentaries and books. What is easy to remember about these three-or-four-point sermons is that each point often has the same letter of the alphabet. For example: Prosperity; Peace; and Purpose.

Very few preachers do expository preaching directly from the Bible. To do expository preaching, a more thorough knowledge of biblical passages is necessary. Ministers realize that a Sunday message is required, and something needs to be done. Is the Lord consulted about what he wants preached?

✤ BIBLICAL ILLITERATES

A majority of those sitting in today's pews, know very little about the Bible. They have little knowledge of whether the words spoken during the sermon are biblical.

It is pathetic that some people who have been in church their entire life don't know or understand the Bible. It's not that they don't read the Bible, for they often have read it throughout their lives. They have been faithful in their devotionals and prayers for a lifetime. But they have never *studied* the Bible. How can this be when they have not only been faithful in reading at home, but also have gone to Bible study at the church as well? Over the years, it became a routine for them. Many of these folks who don't know the Bible are teachers as well.

On worship days at some churches, teachers pick-and-choose what they teach during what is called *"Bible Study"* or the *"Sunday School Hour."* Instead of teaching the Bible, some teach books by well-known authors or teach from commentaries written by denomination scholars. In fact, some churches use this time to critique a book written by a well-known author. Churches are not book clubs but are to preach God's teachings and God's ways.

After graduating from the seminary, I became aware of a colleague who, without any preparation, took a concordance into his pulpit on Sunday morning and preached from its pages. He was a godly man who expected revival every Sunday. The practice of unpreparedness is not recommended to anyone.

✢ TEACHERS/MINISTERS

According to the Bible there is a difference between a minister and a teacher. All Christians are priests.

> "You also, like living stones, are being built into a spiritual house to be a holy priesthood, offering spiritual sacrifices acceptable to God through Jesus Christ" (1 Peter 2:5).

Please note that I used the word "Christian" above. The word "Christian" is mentioned three times in the New Testament and its meaning is "belonging to Christ." Regardless of the claims of many to be Christians, those outside the church need to know that not all churchgoing people are Christians. "Christian" *is* a word that is used very loosely in America. One can test this by asking someone you might meet on the street or wherever, if they are a Christian. An answer might be "I hope so," or "I think that I am."

God gives talents to all Christians. Some Christians will use their talents, and some won't. To a Christian teacher he gives the knowledge and the wisdom to teach the Bible. Teachers will get caught up in using supportive Bible study material published by their denomination. Often, their teaching will be derived from denominational published material that are not necessarily Bible oriented. The Bible is to be properly interpreted by the denomination and not be used for the promotion of a denominational belief.

Search the scriptures for the truth of God.

> "All Scripture is God-breathed and is useful for teaching, rebuking, correcting and training in righteousness, so that the servant of God may be thoroughly equipped for every good work" (2 Tim. 3: 16-17).

Churches will be closing when the Word of God is not being taught nor preached within its walls.

When ministers or teachers tell you that the Bible was written centuries ago and that certain scriptures don't apply for today's society, one should know that the Word is not being taught. The best advice is to seek another minister or teacher.

✢ REVERENDS

A form of the word *"reverend"* is used only one time in the entire KJV Bible. It describes God's name.

> He sent redemption unto his people: he hath commanded his covenant for ever: holy and reverend is his name (Psalm 111: 9).

In the NIV, *"reverent"* is translated as 'awesome.' He provided redemption for his people; he ordained his covenant forever - holy and awesome is his name. The use of these two words refers to the Lord God.

"Reverend" is loosely used today in addressing ministers or preachers. Some ministers deplore being addressed as reverend and desire the use of the word, "Pastor," while some gleefully love being addressed as reverend.

Matthew 23: 8-11, has this to say about titles:

> "But you are not to be called 'Rabbi,' for you
> have one Teacher, and you are all brothers. And
> do not call anyone on earth 'father,' for you have
> one Father, and he is in heaven. Nor are you to
> be called instructors, for you have one Instructor,
> the Messiah. The greatest among you will be your
> servant. For those who exalt themselves will be
> humbled, and those who humble themselves will
> be exalted."

Years ago, service stations pumped the gas for you. These service stations which once advertised *"full service"* have been replaced by *convenience stores* where you pump your own gas. (A sad similarity to what churches is being turned into this day and time.) When these *full serviced* stations existed, some ministers placed a symbol of clergy near their gasoline cap - thinking that they might be offered a discount for their purchase.

Some well-known men in America use the title "Reverend" to make their living. They don't stand in pulpits and don't serve churches, but relish in the title which they use. These Reverends are politicians, activists, and CEO's of fund-raising corporations. Many will go to extremes by adding the "Right Reverend" or the "Right Reverend Doctor" to their name.

We often accuse attorneys of being first on the scene when accidents, disasters, deaths or any profit-making activity occurs. These "reverends" are guilty of this. They come and stand with victims or families before the cameras of the media for another dollar is in the making. The more recognition they can receive from supposedly comforting the downhearted, the more money is going to end up in their wallets. Watch the next disaster or shooting to see the reverends who are enriched by their appearance.

CHAPTER TWENTY-SEVEN

A TOUCHY SUBJECT ABOUT MINISTERS

✣ TRUTH OR FICTION

A TOUCHY SUBJECT? BECAUSE IT MIGHT DESCRIBE SOME pulpiteers which you may know. Being a minister, the finger may point back to me.

Some ministers are under the impression that they are God's gift to society. According to some, they have left the business world's highest paying jobs and could be making much more money than they are presently being paid. However, some of the more financially laden churches have made some of them millionaires.

> Be shepherds of God's flock that is under your care, watching over them - not because you must, but because you are willing, as God wants you to be; not pursuing dishonest gain, but eager to serve; not lording it over those entrusted to you, but being examples to the flock (1 Peter 5:2-3).

Some will gladly talk from the pulpit about the sacrifices which they have made in serving the Lord.

✧ FAVORTISM

Some ministers allow and permit members of their congregations to adore them instead of God. Parishioners place their leaders on a high pedestal. They expect them to be godlier than they are. This expectation becomes a welcoming moment for some pastors. Instead, the minister should become a Barney Fife by *"nipping it in the bud."*

To serve a church as its shepherd and leader, a pastor will wholeheartedly love all the people and not just those who cater to his wishes. Congregations are to be loved more than the worldly hobbies and interests which so easily attracts the pastor's attention and interferes with his ministry.

Churches which call ministers to be their shepherds, will express their need for a godly man as their shepherd: a minister who will preach the Word. Pastors are to put aside their desires, friends, interests, even family if necessary, and the interests which previously captured their attention. Jesus says,

> "If anyone comes to me and does not hate father and mother, wife and children, brother and sister - yes, even their own life - such a person cannot be my disciple" (Luke 14: 26).

All Christians are disciples. A minister is also a disciple.

This verse needs a lot of explaining. A pastor is on a work schedule each week and so are the parishioners whom he is serving. Parishioners want an example of his love to them. What is being preached from the pulpit is the way which he is living his life. He is willing to do and is doing what he is asking them to do. Rightly, they want to see a sermon - rather than hearing one.

In 1858, Abraham Lincoln said, "You can fool all the people some of the time and some of the people all the time, but you cannot fool all the people all the time." Years often go by before the truth will come out.

✝ EXTRA-MARTIAL RELATIONSHIPS

A pastor in central Florida, serving a large church for some twenty years, made a confession at a Wednesday night prayer meeting: he and the secretary at the church had been in a sexual relationship for years. He asked the church for forgiveness and for his ministry to continue. Christian believers are forgiving people, knowing that they were sinners who have been forgiven by the grace of God. Whether he should have is questionable. Instead of the pastor resigning and leaving the church, the secretary was asked to leave.

✝ PASTORING

Many pastor's homilies are shaped around pleasing those members who give them lavish praises and who constantly seek the minister's attention. It's a return to the past elementary school teacher's pet days.

In many sermons, more quotes come from commentaries and authors of published books than from the Bible. Catered to members often will quote more from what is said by the minister than from the Scriptures.

Vocationally called preachers are fearful of allowing anyone to fill their pulpits in their absence. It could be a risk of their job and authority should members like the substitute better. Though they might have other ministers on their staff, they will invite professors from colleges or seminaries to fill in during their absence.

These invited professors who have chosen teaching as their occupation are not God called pastors or they would be pastoring. Some have been ordained as ministers but feel the call to teach as a profession. If they were God-called ministers they would be serving in that capacity. In most instances, (unless they have been gifted by God to preach and to teach) they remain teachers when they stand to preach God's Word. Some churches prefer a *teaching* minister instead of a *preaching* one.

> So Christ himself gave the apostles, the prophets, the evangelists, the pastors and teachers, to equip his people for works of service, so that the body of Christ may be built up (Eph. 4: 11-12).

A member knows if he is considered a part of the flock or if he is cared about by the way the minister will acknowledge him. Some will pass you in the hallway and never acknowledge your presence or give you a greeting. They will rush by you to enter the presence of those with whom, perhaps, they feel more comfortable.

It's very similar to the parable of the Good Samaritan (Luke 10: 25-37) when the priest and the Levite passed by on the other side of the road. The two religious leader's motives to past by on the other side of the road is not explained by Jesus in this parable. The reason for a minister to ignore some parishioners while giving more attention to others, remains a mystery.

Some will act like a big fish in a small pond and wish to be the chief rooster in the hen house. Their egos will accept nothing less than the full attention of others.

Almost all ministers preach forgiveness from the Bible, but some don't practice it when being confronted by others. One minister I know refused to serve on a volunteer team because he had a previous argument with a person which was on the team. He was not humble in his approach. It had to be his way or the highway. Forgiveness was not in his vocabulary on this occasion and perhaps had never been.

✠ REMAINING ON BOARD

Some ministers, after retirement, will not leave the church to attend another one across town. They refuse to leave yesterday behind and to forget that they are no longer the shepherd of the flock. Thinking they know what is best for the church, they still want their voice to be heard. Others want to be seen, praised, recognized and even adored. Many will rest on their laurels instead of giving glory and praise to the heavenly Father.

I was taught while at the seminary that a minister should never remain on the church field where he once pastored. General Douglas MacArthur in his farewell address said, *"Old soldiers never die they just fade away."* Perhaps it's best for some churches where ministers once served if they don't remain. The teaching at the seminary is not based on scripture and was based on prior problems in some churches.

On a recent trip to New England, a family member confessed that in the church which she was attending there was a problem. A new pastor was coming to her Lutheran church due to the retirement of the present pastor. The problem was that the retiring minister wanted to remain a member where he had served for years. According to the church's by-laws or the by-laws of the Lutherans, it wasn't permitted for former pastors to remain on the field where they once served. Many denominational churches have the same problem. It could be a blessing for a newly arriving pastor, since he wouldn't have to hear from some members about the way Rev. Doe did things.

I'm being harsh in my personal descriptive manner of viewing ministers in a judgmental way. I've described some of the characteristics of those whom I've known or been familiar with over the years. If some ministers who are readers of this book, whether God-called or vocationally called, will do what is best for the Lord's work, then the purpose has been accomplished.

✠ FALSE PROPHETS

Should a defense of my writings be needed, let's return to the Scriptures. Jesus says,

> "Watch out for false prophets." They come to you in sheep's clothing, but inwardly they are ferocious wolves. By their fruits you will recognize them (Matt 7: 15-16a).

For some God-called ministers who preach to benefit those who cater to them, the Scriptures has this to say:

> When Cephas came to Antioch, I opposed him to his face, because he stood condemned. For before certain men came from James, he used to eat with the Gentiles. But when they arrived, he began to draw back and separate himself from the Gentiles because he was afraid of those who belonged to the circumcision group. The other Jews joined him in his hypocrisy, so that by their hypocrisy even Barnabas was led astray (Gal. 2: 11-13).

These words by the apostle Paul are condemnation words to not only the Apostle Peter but to every minister who is called by God to preach to the masses and to live according to his calling. It becomes easy to get sidetracked in one's ministry. Whether one is called by God or vocationally called, the message from the pulpit is about the good news of the gospel and the pulpit is to be used: to reach out to the lost and a building up of the saints.

Apply this precept to a secular vocation: A person working in the work-a-day world is employed and paid to support the company and products which are being prepared to go on the marketplace. Their chief purpose is to promote their employer's interests and not to promote the interests of a competitor. A minister representing a church is called to preach God's message from the Bible. The devil has many within the church doing his work.

This is one of the reasons why **THE KILLING OF THE CHRISTIAN CHURCH IN AMERICA** is happening. Many in the ministry have their own agenda and the gospel of Christ Jesus is not being preached.

I have set through many sermons and heard everything from how to get rid of ants and to why not to wash your hands for forty-five seconds after wiping them with GermX. I have listened to weather reports and reports about army worms. I have heard the Scriptures read and then not preached. I have sat through redundant homilies from twenty-five minutes to an hour in length in which Jesus was not once mentioned. So, why is Christianity on the decline in America? The church is not hearing the gospel of our Lord.

✢ THE ENTERTAINERS

At a recent funeral where the respectful mourners had gathered, the less than sixty-year-old officiating minister told the assembled that he had preached *"hundreds and hundreds and hundreds"* of funerals. At the beginning of the service, he declared that this would be an unusual service. The reason for its unusualness was that it was prophetic in nature. And, since it was unique and prophetic, it would be a first-time experience for us listeners.

Two or three verses were read from the Holy Bible pertaining to the *"his star"* which the wise men followed to the stable where Jesus was born. Of course, that was Jesus' star, but today, the deceased became the *"star"* and we were to follow *"her star"* (life) in order to get to our eternal home of heaven. It's respectful to honor the deceased, but no one take the place of Jesus.

The officiating minister had lost his credibility as a minister long before his one-hour discourse ended. Do listeners discern and evaluate what they are hearing from pulpits across these United States of America? Why are we willing to accept such rhetoric from a pulpit that supposedly is on holy ground?

Every year, fewer and fewer Americans are not claiming any religious affiliation. According to a Pew Research Poll in 1990, 86% of adults identified as Christians. In 2008, this figure had fallen to 76%.

Millennials and other young adults, even up to the middle aged, are becoming less affiliated with religion as they get older. A survey in 2007, revealed that 34% of millennials born during the years of 1981–1989, were religiously unaffiliated. As polls are conducted, they reveal that the interest in religion continues to decline.

It's difficult to determine how much of this declining membership in Christian churches across America can be attributable to ministers who are standing behind pulpits in America.

CHAPTER TWENTY-EIGHT

CHURCH LEADERS

✢ DEACONS/ELDERS

SOME DENOMINATIONAL CHURCHES HAVE BOTH deacons and elders. Other churches might have deacons only while some churches might have elders and not deacons. Some believe that the Bible calls for elders, while others understand the deacons and elders to be the same.

Frankly, whether it's elders and deacons or elders or deacons is of little importance to me. There isn't a reason to split a church over such issues. Some, however, will question that. What matters, however, is how the church will use these appointed individuals. There is a purpose and calling for deacons or else why have them?

During my ministry, the churches which I have pastored had deacons and no elders. The deacons usually gathered with me before the preaching service on Sunday mornings. We prayed together before entering the sanctuary. And upon entering the sanctuary, the deacons entered with me and would sit together in a front-row pew. This may sound like the old time use of *"mourning"* or *"moaning"* benches but wasn't. This assembling and sitting together of the deacons during the worship hour was traditional for churches at that time. Some churches might still be doing it today.

✚ ALTAR CALLS

Across America today, you will find few, if any, churches having *"mourning"* or *"moaning"* benches. But, in years-gone-by, a small pew at the front of the church was used during regular meetings and revivals for repentant sinners whether saved or unsaved.

These repentant sinners would make their way down the aisles to sit on this designated bench. The bench was used for other functions as well - even for a repentant church member who had gone astray and was now coming to confess their sins and ask for the forgiveness of the church.

This practice was new at the time and was used in a repentant way. It was a way in which sinners could confess and acknowledge their sinfulness before God and the church. The Bible teaches of "confessing your sins before others." It brought members closer together by sharing their needs with others. More of this will bring the church closer by acknowledging our sins before others and asking for the prayers of the church.

"Therefore, confess your sins to each other and pray for each other so that you may be healed. The prayer of a righteous person is powerful and effective" (James 5: 16).

The following lyrics is a traditional Gospel song dating from 1873. It was included in a list of Jubilee songs.

"Give me that old time religion
Tis the old-time religion
And it's good enough for me.
It was good for our mothers.
Makes me love everybody,
It has saved our fathers,
It will do when I am dying.
It will take us all to heaven.

Copied from Lyrics @ Warner/Chappell Music. Lyrics Licensed and provided by LyricsFind. This old song was used by many old-timers, especially in revivals and brush arbor settings of the past. Jesus is not mentioned in the above lyrics, but saved folks knew back then and even now, that the only path to Heaven is through Jesus.

"Mourning" or *"moaning"* benches have all but disappeared from denominational churches and been replaced by altar calls. Roman Catholics have their confessional booths. The routine of deacons making their unison appearance with a minister before the traditional morning service has also disappeared.

✢ CONFESSION IS GOOD FOR THE SOUL

I am familiar with a young woman who was a member of a congregation in a town distant from the church which she now attends. While on the previous church's roll, she had a baby out of wedlock. Leaving the church, she joined a body of believers in another town. Later, she was convicted by the Holy Spirit and was ashamed of her previous sinful actions. It was on her mind constantly that she needed to go back to her former church, stand before the assembly, and ask for their forgiveness. The joy and peace of the Lord returned in her life when she confessed her transgression to her former church and asked for their forgiveness.

✢ DUTIES AND RESPONSIBILITIES

Deacons and elders have certain duties within the church. They are to perform certain responsibilities:

> "So the Twelve gathered all the disciples together and said, "it would not be right for us to neglect the ministry of the word of God in order to wait on tables. Brothers and sisters, choose seven men from among you who are known to be full of the Spirit and wisdom. We will turn this responsibility over

to them and will give our attention to prayer and
the ministry of the word" (Acts: 6: 2-4).

Seven men were chosen from among them to perform a
fair distribution of food which was to be made to widows of
the Hellenistic Jews and Hebraic Jews.

In today's culture, the performance of a fair distribution
of food isn't needed in America. While a fair distribution of
food to widows was a practice of that day, it doesn't openly
exist today in this country. However, widows are still with us,
and they have varied needs. Today's deacons and elders are to
minister to whatever the needs of widows are within Christian
churches. Otherwise, why do churches ordain deacons unless
there are existing widow needs within the church? Some
deacons within some denominations, become more involved
with the administration of the church rather than ministering
to the needs of widows and the membership.

> In the same way, deacons are to be worthy of
> respect, sincere, not indulging in much wine,
> and not pursuing dishonest gain. They must keep
> hold of the deep truths of the faith with a clear
> conscience. They must first be tested and then
> if there is nothing against them, let them serve
> as deacons. In the same way, the women are to
> be worthy of respect, not malicious talkers but
> temperate and trustworthy in everything. A deacon
> must be faithful to his wife and must manage his
> children and his household well. Those who have
> served well gain an excellent standing and great
> assurance in their faith in Christ Jesus (1 Tim. 3:
> 8-13).

You will note in the previous quotation from Scripture
the passage which reads, "In the same way, the women are to
be worthy of respect, not malicious talkers but temperate and

trustworthy in everything." It is unclear to biblical scholars as to whether this sentence is saying that women in the church can become deacons or whether this is to be interpreted to mean that the women who are the wives of deacons. According to some biblical scholars, it could go either way. From my reading and study of this passage and being in the context of what is expected of deacons, the women mentioned are the wives of deacons. In Romans, chapter 16, verse 1, Phoebe is called a deacon and not a deaconess in Greek.

Among the seven men who became the first deacons, Stephen and Philip took upon themselves the ministry of preaching. There are other functions which deacons may be qualified in doing. Stephen and Philip were commissioned as deacons, but they took on additional responsibilities other than the serving of tables to the widows. The other five deacons in the Book of Acts are never mentioned again. Dr. Luke, the writer of Acts, focused on the ministry of Stephen and Philip.

It appears that some deacons who are ordained and commissioned to the office of a deacon today, are like the five who disappeared from the print of the Bible. Their role as a deacon becomes only a prestigious title which sets them apart from others within the church. Deacons have their meetings, but some appear hesitant in administering to the needs of those within the church with specific needs. In Acts, most of the apostles and deacons disappear from scriptures. Dr. Luke appears to focus his attention on those who were with him on some of his journeys.

Personally, I have met some godly deacons and some ungodly ones. Many deacons outweigh me by tons with respect to their tasks. Many have supported me in my decisions and even in my wrongness. Many have kept their thoughts and opinions to themselves when they should have been more open. They have lifted me up in their prayers. Godly deacons, I have found, are the men who love the Lord God and His Word. These deacons have been gifted by God and true to their calling.

But not all deacons keep silent. One deacon, who couldn't keep quiet in his anger was anxious to confess his anger to me. "You have driven a wedge between me and you, he said. 'Do you know what a wedge is?' he asked.

'*Yes,*' I responded.

He, being skilled in carpentry, wasn't sure that I knew what a wedge was and went further to clarify the purpose of a wedge. "A wedge is driven into something or a piece of wood with no intention of having it ever removed. You have driven a wedge between us. It will never be removed."

He was being honest with me. However, I might have been guilty of provoking his anger, but I wasn't the one who had driven the wedge. He continued his deaconship, and I continued as his pastor. We never had the same conversation again.

✢ ELDERS/OVERSEERS

> Here is a trustworthy saying. Whoever aspires to be an overseer desires a noble task. Now the overseer is to be above reproach, faithful to his wife, temperate, self-controlled, respectable, hospitable, able to teach, not given to drunkenness, not violent but gentle, not quarrelsome, not a lover of money. He must manage his own family well and see that his children obey him, and he must do so in a manner worthy of full respect. (If anyone does not know how to manage his own family, how can he take care of God's church?) He must not be a recent convert, or he may become conceited and fall under the same judgment as the devil. He must also have a good reputation with outsiders, so that he will not fall into disgrace and into the devil's trap (1 Tim. 3: 1-7).

The Holy Word of God speaks of the office of deacons, overseers and elders. The assumption by some scholars when thinking of elders, is that this is an older adult. But that is not necessarily true. In the New Testament, all elders are older people, but not all older people are elders. I have never been a member of a church where all three roles were active. Some churches decide on whether they will have deacons or elders.

In those churches, the shepherd of the church becomes the senior elder. The desire of many pastors is to be totally in control of every function within the church. Whether the elders are young or old, elected elders will need the approval of the senior elder.

Every Bible reader and student of the Word of God should know and understand that Jesus is the Chief Shepherd. The Holy Spirit of God is the One who does the granting of gifts and talents to the membership.

Some denominational churches are autonomous bodies with their own bylaws. It's also the responsibility of deacons, overseers and elders to see that the bylaws of the church are being carried out.

Churches exist for one purpose:

> "Therefore go and make disciples of all nations, baptizing them in the name of the Father and of the Son and of the Holy Spirit, and teaching them to obey everything I have commanded you. And surely I am with you always, to the end of the age" (Matt. 28: 19-20).

Churches and their leaders across America have lost sight of their sole existing purpose to make disciples. Church leaders, whether pastors, deacons, overseers or elders, aren't in office to feed their appetites. But they are to fulfill the purpose for their existence.

"Be careful not to practice your righteousness in front of others to be seen by them. If you do, you will have no reward from your Father in heaven" (Matt. 6: 1).

CHAPTER TWENTY-NINE

TEACHERS

✢ TEACHING: A GOD GIVEN GIFT

> And God has placed in the church first of all apostles, second prophets, third teachers, then miracles, then gifts of healing, of helping, of guidance, and of different kinds of tongues" (1 Cor. 12: 28).

UNKNOWN NUMBER OF TEACHERS WITHIN ANY CHURCH are not God-called, gifted teachers but have been placed in that position to fill a role or a need. Some of these self-proclaimed teachers are teaching because the church has no one else to fill the void. Some church members step forward to fill an existing vacancy because there is no one to fill the need. According to Scripture, teaching and helping are two different responsibilities.

Gone are the days when Christian churches had more teachers than needed. In the early 1960s, there was a church in the New Orleans area which would not permit a teacher to teach on Sunday unless they attended a Wednesday Bible study class where the lesson for the coming Sunday was taught. I wonder if such a requirement still exists at this church today.

The Bible says that *helping* is also a gifting by God. These helpers can be substitutes filling in for an absentee teacher or where there is an existing need. A helper can only reach certain heights in the teaching of God's word.

Teaching Sunday after Sunday for years doesn't make a God-called teacher neither does years of experience and neither does the knowledge of the Bible. The gift of teaching comes only through the Holy Spirit of God giving this gift.

You will find all kinds and types of teachings in denominational churches. You will find those who put their personality and chemistry into their teaching. These efforts at teaching are characterized as being dramatic, historic, dynamic, poetic, and/or graphic. Each teacher has a unique personality. Some listeners instantly become followers or disciples of the teacher. We are not to become followers of any individual.

> "What I mean is this: One of you says, "I follow Paul," another, "I follow Apollos," another, "I follow Cephas," still another, "I follow Christ" (1 Cor. 1:12).

Jesus is the One to be followed.

Listeners cater to certain types of teachers. Some students of the Bible like more in-depth studies than what is being taught in the Bible study periods at their church. Some teachers will go to great length in preparing their lessons. Some will teach from concordances, Bible study materials offered by their denominations, devotional books and/or pamphlets. Some teachers have become desperate in their attempts to appease their listeners and will resort to materials which do not pertain to the Bible.

In smaller churches, there might be only two classes of Bible study - one for the adults and one for the children. Whereas, in larger churches, adults and children are divided by their ages and/or interests.

In many cases, the leadership of the church is unaware as to what is being taught in so-called Bible study classes. Bible studies are seldom monitored by those who are in leadership positions.

The reason for many teachers leaving the Bible and teaching what they are more comfortable with is that they are not spiritually led by the task before them. Teaching the Bible can become a storytelling process where there isn't any spirituality.

Parents who teach Bible character stories at home to their children use them often as bedtime stories and don't teach them in a spiritual way. This opportunity to teach the Bible at home is a very good way for parents to implant in the minds of their children the teachings of God's Word. The Holy Spirit will come alongside and use the parents or the Bible stories for conviction and conversion.

✢ PREACHERS AND THEIR ROLE

All God called ministers are gifted by the Holy Spirit for either preaching or teaching. Some ministers are teachers and not preachers. Whereas, some ministers are preachers and not teachers.

A preacher's fantasy to please their listeners will become an obstacle to the preaching and teaching of God's message.

How many preachers in their preparation to stand before others ask God in advance, "Lord, what is your message for these people?" "Will it be my message or God's message?"

Jesus pronounced seven woes on the Pharisees, a religious party, in Matthew, Chapter 23, about their teachings. For brevity sake, only a couple of verses will be listed.

> "Woe to you, teachers of the law and Pharisees, you hypocrites! You give a tenth of your spices - mint, dill and cumin. But you have neglected the more important matters of the law - justice, mercy, and faithfulness. You should have practiced the latter without neglecting the former. You blind guides! You strain out a gnat but swallow a camel" (Matt. 23: 23-24).

CHAPTER THIRTY

FAITH OR UNBELIEF

✢ ATHEIST/AGNOSTIC

WHO IS PREACHING FROM YOUR CHURCH'S PULPIT today? Is he or she a believer or an unbeliever? We want to believe every one of them is a believer. Church members would be insulted if such a question were asked of them. But, nevertheless, what does your pulpiteer believe?

Clergymen, ministers, preachers and priests that are being heard across America, whether on Saturdays, Sundays or throughout the week, may be an atheist or an agnostic. Such a person could be standing in the pulpit in your church this Sunday.

"Absurd," one might respond.

✢ IF NOT ASKED/DON'T TELL

I once read a story about a student in a theological institution who was an atheist. Upon his graduation, the young man asked for ordination. The professors knew of his unbelief and asked him if he was still an unbeliever. "Yes," he responded. He was then asked if he had told his church about his unbelief. "No," he said. *"Good, don't tell them."* They went ahead with the ordination. This story might sound farfetched to my readers. If I could remember the source of this story, I would like to give them credit for this information, but it is true of so many ministers who are unbelievers.

Why would a person be in a vocation which talks about the existence of a God which he doesn't personally believe in or have serious doubts about? And, why would a salesperson in any occupation represent an item or a product which he or she does not believe to be good? For some, their job is only a livelihood. They desire monetary profit. Why then, shouldn't a person preach something in which he doesn't believe in to make a living? Who becomes the guilty party, the unbeliever or his congregation?

Atheists who preach from Christian pulpits justify their actions by saying: "I'm not to blame. They want a message from the Bible, so that's what I'm giving them. I read from the Bible, expound a little, and they are satisfied. I give them what they want to hear. I don't have to say that I believe it just by having read or quoted it."

There are untold numbers of preachers who have left the Christian ministry and declared that they don't believe there is a God. Some have formed their own fellowship gatherings.

There was a woman who was an admitted atheist, who was a frequent visitor at a church which I pastored in the state of Washington. She was especially open to me about her lack of belief in God. But to my knowledge, she did not confess to anyone else. She never participated in any other function of the church except attending the Sunday morning worship service. There was no talking or persuasion that would change her thinking. Undoubtedly, she came for the fellowship or to get out of her surroundings. Or sent by the devil's advocates to convert me to her way of thinking.

✣ PASTORS DECLARING ATHEISM

As mentioned previously, untold numbers have left the Christian ministry due to their unbelief in the existence of God. Some atheists are still preaching in Christian churches where even some of their parishioners are aware of their unbelief.

If the truth were known, there are so many unbelievers in churches who are not scripturally oriented to know the difference between an atheist and a true man of the cloth.

Ministers leaving their Christian fellowships and declaring atheism meet often with other atheist ministers for fellowship. They are still seeking to fill the existing voids in their lives.

On a business trip years ago, I registered at a large hotel in downtown Atlanta. Many of the rooms and the convention hall within the hotel were dedicated to a convention for devil worshippers from different states. It wasn't October 31st, but some tourists might have thought that a Halloween party was taking place

Some few years ago, the New York Times published an article titled, "From Bible-Belt Pastor to Atheist Leader." The article was about Jerry DeWitt, an atheist convert from DeRidder, LA. According to the article, Mr. DeWitt, having been in the Christian ministry for some twenty-five years and having served two evangelical churches, converted to atheism. He is now going around the country preaching the non-existence of God. His name is very well-known among atheists and agnostics.

According to this New York Times' article, Mr. Dewitt's conversion to atheism came after a call from a woman asking for prayer for her brother who had been in a motorcycle accident. But the words for prayer would not come. Sobbing and searching, he could only console the woman. This experience started him on a path of research for or with existing atheist groups. And, there are many of them.

There are names for many of these organizations and there are many well-known people, according to the New York Times article: Sam Harris, Daniel Dennett, Christopher Hitchens and Richard Dawkins are known as the *"4 Horsemen."* These are the best-known evangelists of the atheistic movement. Atheists have their own language, a glossary borrowed from Alcoholics Anonymous, the Bible and gay liberation. People always "come out" of the atheist closet.

Readers might well remember the name of Madalyn Murray O'Hair. Due to her large number of lawsuits, she became known, "as the most hated woman in America."

These atheist organizations are on the move in spreading their doctrine throughout the world and in rendering aid to ex-clergymen if needed. Some of these organizations are known as: "Clergy Project;" "Recovering from Religion;" "United Coalition of Reason;" and "Secular Student Alliance." There are many more agencies and movements in existence to further atheism and agnosticism.

✢ ATHEISM IN MANY LEARNING INSTITUTIONS

A very disturbing fad is that high schools, colleges, universities and seminaries are being infiltrated by those who are promoting such beliefs. Some educational facilities are being asked by students for permission to have their own atheist clubs. Sons and daughters of churchgoers, who were brought up in the church, and may have become church members due to persuasion by their parents are now turning away from God's Word. A growing number of young people are moving away from godliness to godlessness. Most of this is attributable to the liberalism within the walls of our educational facilities and to environmental exposures outside the Christian home.

This movement on the part of a younger generation can be attributed to parents not teaching the Bible at home, to churches having failed in their efforts and to parents and church members failure to display Christian principles in the way in which they live their lives before these children.

It is doubtful that this is just a rebellious movement on the part of the young now that they are out of sight of home. All of us would like to put the blame somewhere outside of our personal domain. As a young person, I wanted to get out of the home, but my motive wasn't rebellious. At that time, I wasn't into the Bible and its teachings. In fact, I didn't have a Bible. I didn't even know what a Christian was. Love for family and their ways taught me right from wrong and how to treat other people.

✣ VERY LITTLE KNOWN ABOUT THE BIBLE

The ones fellowshipping within the confines of denominational churches each week don't pick up a Bible during the week. Very little is known about the Bible and what the Bible has to say. These lackadaisical church members are not aware of whether a homily is biblical or not. Church attending has become a routine which is lacking a spiritual context. Churchgoers come and leave as empty as when they sat down in the pew. Those believers or unbelievers who aren't familiar with the Bible will certainly not know how to live the Bible before others during the week.

I have heard it said, "A church member can rise no higher spiritually than his shepherd *or* leader." There is more truth in that statement than fiction. A leader, who is not spiritually led, will pull down spiritually led members of a flock. Spiritual hunger exists in the hearts of everyone. Christians need to be fed. It's impossible for a non-spiritual person to lead anyone in drinking of the water and the eating the food of the Lord God.

Under the leadership of church leaders, who don't have a calling of God and a message from God, members will continue to leave churches seeking other venues never to return. "Ignorance of the law is no excuse," as courts say. Neither is ignorance of what God says through his Word an excuse.

The Lord God has had enough of people's ignorance.

CHAPTER THIRTY-ONE

INSTITUTIONS OF HIGHER LEARNING

✢ BRAINWASHING

PARENTS TODAY WITH A SON OR DAUGHTER IN A learning institution should be extremely concerned about what their children are being taught. Many millions or our young people are being brainwashed. Covert and overt tactics are being used at these institutions.

Brainwashing is removing the values which have been taught previously by family members or Christians institutions and replacing them by putting into one's minds the beliefs of others. It's an old technique which has been used for ages, especially during wars and conflicts.

Families have lost their togetherness and their values over these recent years. There isn't a desire by multitudes for a return to the values taught during childhood. During the first three years of a person's life many values are instilled. Outside the home, many seeds are being planted to erase from our minds instilled values.

Over the years, I have returned to my old homestead just to reminisce. It enables me to leave the present conditions and consequences of a troubled and messed-up world of divisiveness, and to return to days which were simpler. It's relaxing just sitting alone in front of an old abandoned dilapidated frame of a house where once family members slept on old feather beds and on pallets placed on the floor. This is one of the ways for me to get away from the rat race of life. And, it's a great opportunity to clear my mind of unwanted pollutive elements.

Those were the days when there were fewer opinions expressed via networks, newspapers, texting, telephones and television. A person's mind was firmly enriched by the values held by family members. Today, within seconds or minutes, news and opinions from almost any location in the entire world can be heard. Hear a speech on television these days, and afterwards a commentator is telling you what the speaker said. The yesterdays were the days when you voted for the person rather than the political party. All of us are being brainwashed into believing what others believe and that their way is the right way.

✣ CHILDHOOD LEARNING

In my early days of learning, my teachers taught reading, writing and arithmetic. They also did their own brainwashing which included God and the Bible. One of my teachers in my earlier years kept a roster of those attending church each week. Each week she called her roll, recording each "yea" or "nay" as to whether we had attended church the previous Sunday.

I was somewhat embarrassed before other class members if my answer was in the negative. Back in the Bible Belt days of the South, before God and prayers were removed from the schools, it appeared that the majority of my teachers were Christians. It's true - nothing remains the same and Christians precepts have been swept out the door.

✣ A CASE OF BRAINWASHING

Here's an obvious case of brainwashing. Deandre Poole, a professor at Florida Atlantic University in the heart of Fort Lauderdale, told his students to write the word, "Jesus" on a piece of paper and to throw it on the floor and "stomp on it." Only one student, Ryan Rotela, refused to stomp.

Twenty of the twenty-three students in attendance signed a statement saying they were not offended by the exercise. It's most likely that they were influenced or afraid of being reprimanded by the administration after witnessing what action was taken on the student who wouldn't stomp. It's highly unlikely in a class of twenty-three students, in a class in the deep South, that the student who refused to stomp was the only Christian in the class. The days of a Christian being persecuted for beliefs have returned. The student who refused to *"stomp on Jesus"* was disciplined not only by the professor, but by the administration at the university for his refusal to stomp and was subjected to expulsion.

After the media became aware of this and it became news, the professor's action was denounced. It was then and only then that the professor was placed on administrative leave by the university - only to be reinstated some six months later. Professor Poole is vice chairman of the Democratic party in his area, and he made the claim that he is highly religious and a devout Christian.

✧ A HIGH SCHOOL SITUATION

This brainwashing begins early in a person's life. Before we enter the secular world – it begins in daycare centers and in the kindergarten stages of early childhood.

Scott Compton, an honors English teacher at Chapin High School in Chapin, South Carolina, was placed on long-term administrative leave for his inappropriate teaching. Trying to justify his actions, he exclaimed, "It simply was a symbolic piece of cloth." Mr. Compton was later fired.

There were those days when many of us thought throwing panties from the windows of dormitories was bad. The term "panty raid" was first coined in 1949. It became the first college craze after World War II. This craze continued into the 1950s and 1960s. Even later, it continued into some of the concerts held by the singer Tom Jones. Women attending the concerts would stand up, pull off their panties, and would toss or give them to the singer.

✛ OUT OF THE SHELTERED HOME

Many of our young people going off to college to get educated, have never been exposed to the world outside of their home and community. They are now being exposed to a liberal and a far-left movement of brainwashing. Some will succumb to peer pressure since community pressure has waned.

Society in America is drifting further away from the teaching about a Living God. Some are of the thinking, "*If it appears good to you, then do it.*" Modern science, cultural changes, urbanization and lukewarm religious beliefs dominate any sense of reasoning. God is taking up less and less space in a person's daily life - especially within denominational churches and the Roman Catholic Church.

Recently, the Roman Catholic Church announced that it would deal with the abuse of its nuns by the priests and bishops. Through the media we hear about these allegations and promised correctional procedures. There is no way of knowing how much of this is swept under the rug to stay there and rot.

When churched young people leave the sheltered home and enter the learning institutions of the world, those who are not firmly entrenched in their faith, begin to flap their wings of freedom. There isn't a parent around to keep an eye out for their infractions. For some, this is their first ungodly exposure to a world tainted by the wiles of the devil.

Some, prior to entering these institutions, began to stray even while in junior and high school classes. During these years of hidden activities (drinking and smoking), those who were testing the waters knew just how far to descend. Away from the restrictions of the home, one can stray further.

One of my family members, having a firm hand on his daughter during her years at home, brought her home at the conclusion of her first term in college. She was more interested in partying than studying. He had kept a keen eye on her when she entered college and hadn't cut the apron strings.

A young person attending these institutions of learning is introduced and exposed to drugs, alcohol, and to promiscuous or illicit sex. Many are unable to withstand the temptations. Some, because of prior teachings, overcome these temptations. It will take years for some young people to come to their senses and return to the prior teachings of home and family. Some never will.

✤ THE *"GOD IS DEAD"* MOVEMENT

The *"God Is Dead"* movement was introduced to Americans through an article written by John T. Elson, the religion editor of the New York Times. The year was 1966 and the article was published during the Judeo-Christian week of Passover and Easter. The article became one of the most famous covers of the Times, causing a huge increase in sales. A radical new way of thinking about God was being presented furthering an age-old conflict between religion and secular ideas in Western Culture.

William Hamilton, a tenured professor at Colgate Rochester Divinity School in 1965, believed the concept of God had run its course. His belief was that civilization now operated on secular principles and churches should help people to learn to care for each other unconditionally with no illusions of going to heaven when they die.

Mr. Hamilton was joined in his *"God Is Dead Movement"* by Thomas J.J. Altizer of Emory University and Paul van Buren of Temple University. These three theologians were constructing a theology without God. This movement by these three had been previously dealt with in an earlier article in the New York Times in 1965.

John Lennon in an off-the-cuff statement in March 1966 made this comment, "the Beatles were more popular than Jesus."

It is very evident that America is drifting away from Christianity. A research of history will testify to that statement. Harvard, Yale, and Princeton all owe their origin to the Gospels. These were all started by Christians. Princeton was once a seminary. The website, www. forerunner.com states that one hundred six (106) of the first one hundred eight (108) schools in America were founded on the Christian faith.

✣ SCIENTISTS

Some historical notes say that Albert Einstein believed in God. However, some say that Einstein believed in a pantheistic God like Barauch Spinoza, not a personal God.

Stephen William Hawkins who died in March 2018, claimed to be an atheist, but after his meeting with Pope Francis came away saying, "Now I believe." This statement refutes the geniuses who say, "Christians are all dumb."

Again, I must now agree with a former president, Barack Hussein Obama, in saying that we are not a Christian nation. Regardless of the numbers professing Christianity, we are no longer illustrating lives that reflect the Lord Jesus. Should this issue be debated, consider asking this question: "If we are a

Christian nation, why are we permitting the things which are happening in the United States?"

It is true that Christians outnumber other world religions. But Christianity is not keeping up with the population growth. Newsweek magazine announced in 2009 the end of Christian America. A Pew Research poll indicated that by the year 2050, Muslims and Christians will almost be of equal size in the world.

✢ UNIVERSITY AND COLLEGE PROFESSORS

Walter E. Williams, a professor of economics at George Mason University, in an article which appeared in the Rocky Mount (NC) Telegram on February 19, 2020, and titled *"Campus Bias, Anti-Americanism Pose Threats,"* wrote about the makeup of those who are teaching in these institutions of higher learning. Here are a few excerpts from Professor Williams article:

> "A recent Pew Research Center survey finds that only half of American adults think colleges and universities are having a positive effect on our nation. The leftward political bias held by faculty members affiliated with the Democratic Party, at most institutions of higher education explains a lot of that disappointment. Professors Mitchell Langbert and Sean Stevens document this bias in 'Partisan Registration and Contributions of Faculty in Flagship Colleges.'
>
> Langbert and Stevens conducted a new study of the political affiliation of 12,372 professors in the two leading private and two leading public colleges in 31 states. For party registration, they found a Democratic to Republican (D:R) ratio of 8.5:1 which varied by rank of institution and region. For

donations to political candidates (using the Federal Election Commission database), they found a D:R ratio of 95:1, with only 22 Republican donors, compared with 2,081 Democratic donors."

The article continues about the loyalty to America of some professors. There was the arrest recently of a Harvard professor on accusations of materially false, fictious and fraudulent statements about work he had done for the Chinese government that seeks to lure American talent to China.

Harvard professors are not the only ones involved with the Chinese. Emory's neuroscientist Li Xiao-Jiang was fired in 2019. Li was charged with lying about his own ties to China. He was part of the same Chinese program as the professor at Harvard.

A University of California, Los Angeles, professor was found guilty by a jury of exporting stolen USA military technology to China. He was convicted in June 26, 2019 on 18 federal charges according to *Newsweek*.

According to NBC, federal prosecutors say that University of Texas professor, Bo Mao, attempted to steal USA technology. He obtained access to protected circuitry by using his position as a professor. His purpose, as reported, was to hand it over to the Chinese telecommunications giant, Huawei.

The true tragedy is that so many Americans are blind to the fact that today's colleges and universities pose a threat on several fronts to the well-being of our nation.

A major threat to Christianity is what some of these ungodly professors are teaching to our young people.

CHAPTER THIRTY-TWO

MILLENNIALS

Millennials are identified as those who have reached adulthood early in the 21st century and are classified as those born in 1982 and approximately twenty years thereafter.

In 2014, the U.S. Census reported 83.5 million millennials, surpassing that of Baby Boomers born from 1946 to 1964, still with a population of 75.4 million. Millennials are now the largest generation represented in the USA.

✢ WHAT ONE ARTICLE SAYS ABOUT MILLENNIALS AND THEIR FAITH

FACTANK on November 23, 2015, reported that Millennials are less religious than older Americans, but just as spiritual. In an article by Becka A. Alper, who is a research associate at the Pew Research Center, she writes:

> "By many measures, Millennials are much less likely than their elders to be religious. For instance, only about half of Millennials (adults who were born between 1981 and 1996), say they believe in God with absolute certainty, and only about four-in-ten Millennials say religion is very important in their lives. By contrast, older generations are much more likely to believe in God and say religion is important to them.

And this lower level of religiosity among Millennials manifests itself not just in what they think, but in what they do. Just 27% of Millennials say they attend religious services on a weekly basis, a substantially lower share than Baby Boomers (38%) and members of the Silent and Greatest generation (51% each). Similarly, a smaller share of Millennials say they pray every day compared with those in older generations."

Ms. Alper in her research of comparing millennials with the Greatest Generation, gives the following statistics:

* Feel a sense of spiritual peace and well-being: Greatest 70%; Millennials (51%)
* Feel a sense of wonder about the universe: Greatest (44%); Millennials (46%)
* Feel a sense of gratitude or thankfulness: Greatest (77%); Millennials (76%)
* Think about the meaning and purpose of life: Greatest (54%) Millennials (55%)

Her research indicates that Millennials are not as religious as older Americans by some measures of religious observance. But, indicates that Millennials are as likely to engage in many spiritual practices. Like older Americans, writes Ms. Alper, more than four-in-ten of these younger adults (46%) say they feel a deep sense of wonder about the universe at least once a week. Likewise, most Millennials say they think about the meaning and purpose of life on a weekly basis (55%), again similar-to older generations.

Her research indicates that roughly three-quarters of Millennials feel a strong sense of gratitude or thankfulness at least weekly (76%). And 51% say they feel a deep sense of spiritual peace and well-being at least once a week.

Her research reveals that older Americans are only slightly more likely than Millennials to say they feel a strong sense of gratitude. Ms. Alper says, "when it comes to feeling spiritual peace and well-being are members of these four older generations more likely than Millennials to answer in the affirmative."

The difference between Millennials and older Americans is not that large on some traditional measures of religious belief, writes Ms. Alper. When it comes to views on the afterlife, the Pew Research Center's article states that two-thirds of Millennials say they believe in heaven, compared with roughly three-quarters of Baby Boomers and members of the Silent generation. And 56% of Millennials believe in the concept of hell, similar-to older age cohorts.

✢ UNDERSTANDING AND DEFINING WORDS

It appears that today's population of researchers, writers, scientists, poll takers, and even religious denominations, have a difficult time in defining the terms "religion," "spirituality" and "Christianity." These three words may mean several things to the populace.

Ask a person, if you dare, if he or she is a Christian. Many would define themselves as Christians because they were reared in a Christian home. Grandma and grandpa or mom and dad were Christians; therefore, some would say, they are Christians because of the belief of their ancestors. Others, might say, they are Christians because they attended church when they were youths or attend church occasionally now.

A feeling of bliss or a special feeling of contentment doesn't mean that one is a spiritual person. There are times, regardless of circumstances, when persons feel moments of contentment. This contentment can come from several factors: job well done; praise from work done well; increase in income.

The rich youthful ruler went to Jesus and asked:

"Teacher, what good thing must I do to get eternal life?" (Matt. 19: 16b)

Jesus told the young ruler that he had to keep the Law of Moses. The young man responded:

"All these I have kept." "What do I still lack?" Jesus answered, "If you want to be perfect, go, sell your possessions and give to the poor, and you will have treasure in heaven. Then come, follow me." "When the young man heard this, he went away sad, because he had great wealth" (Matt. 19: 20-22).

Many will turn away from Jesus, not because they are rich, but because their lifestyles conflict with the teachings of the Bible. The choice of masses today is to choose a life of living only for themselves.

There is a way that appears to be right, but in the end, it leads to death (Prov. 14:12).

The sad state of mind of multitudes today is that the populace is confused about the meanings of the word "religion," "Christian," "spirituality" and "good works." Many will say being religious is the same as being a Christian. Some will classify themselves as religious people. Others will define themselves as Christians because they live by their good works and relationships with others. While others will regard their attending church as making them religious persons or Christians.

Today's Christians are living with a *"middle of the road"* attitude when it comes to defining Christianity.

✣ POLITICS AND MOVEMENTS

Millennials, in most cases, want to be a part of something. They wish to make their voices heard as they seek ways to make their imprint on society. Encouraged by their professors and peers, they soon become active in politics and movements.

It's an election year, and millennials who are seeking higher education are being promised by some politicians of tuition free education. For those who have student loans, their debts will be forgiven.

Throughout history, people have sold their votes for money by being told how to vote. What is the difference between receiving money for the way you voted or being promised future possibilities after graduation of having a clean slate?

We have all been young at some stage in life. What sounded good to us at those times of youngness were what would make our lives complete. As young folks, one will lean toward the thinking of those who are seeking their own ambitions.

May our young people been taught godliness at home and not be led by others who are making promises of things which are too good to be true.

CHAPTER THIRTY-THREE

THE MEDIA

✢ SHAPING THE MINDS OF THE PUBLIC

TIME, WHOSE CIRCULATION HAS BEEN TANKING FOR years, is still read by millions and have more liberal readers than conservatives. Their columnists are liberal minded. The following article contains some truths, but it is slanted by the writer to appease its liberal and politically left audience. Many articles in TIME never tell "the truth, the whole truth and nothing but the truth." Liberal newsprint, when it pertains to non-liberal politicians, features only the worst about the person and nothing about the good.

I am a subscriber to TIME magazine and the following article dated (July 8, 2019) by David French, entitled "The Evangelical Republic of Fear" appeared: (Because of length, only a portion of this article is stated verbatim.)

> "...The relentless drumbeat of claims against Trump—combined with the clear moral declaration of the past—have caused millions of Americans to look at their evangelical fellow citizens and ask, simply: Why? Why have you abandoned your previous commitment to political character to embrace Donald Trump.
>
> Part of the explanation is undeniably basic partisanship and ambition. White evangelicals are largely Republican, and they're generally going to vote for Republicans. And proximity to power has

always had it attractions for religious charlatans of all stripes. But I'd suggest the real reason for the breadth and depth of evangelical support is deeper and—perversely—even more destructive to its religious witness.

That reason is fear.

Personally, I don't believe in a large percentage of his lengthy article or opinions. The Holy Bible states many times God's words when he says, "Fear not, I will be with you."

Mr. French contrasts President Trump's sexual acts with those of former president, Bill Clinton. Sin, as Christians know it, means to miss the mark of God's calling. These two presidents have sinned. Which one's sin is the greater? Sin is sin.

In my opinion, the fear which Mr. French is writing about, is that Christians feared Mrs. Clinton's policies more than they did the policies of Mr. Trump. This is to say that Christians feared that certain constitutional rights would be taken away.

The writer believes that fear is all too often a dominant theme of their political life and the church is under siege from a hostile culture.

Mr. French lists some reasons for this supposed *fear* among evangelicals:

* Religious institutions are under legal attack from progressives.
* The left wants nuns to facilitate access to abortifacients and contraceptives,
* The left wants Christian adoption agencies to compromise their conscience or close.
* Casts doubt about tax exemptions of religious education institutions if they adhere to traditional Christian sexual ethics.

Mr. French believes that millions of young Christians from the early days of Sunday school, were taught the biblical verse:

'For God gave us not a spirit of fear but of power and love and self-control.'

In 2016, Mr. French believes that something snapped. "I saw Christian men and women whom I've known and respected for years respond with raw fear at the very idea of a Hillary Clinton presidency. They believed she was going to place the church in mortal danger. The Christian writer Eric Metaxas wrote that if Hillary won, America's chance to have a 'Supreme Court that values the Constitution' will be 'gone.' 'Not for four years, not for eight,' he said, 'but forever.' These were the words of fearful men grasping at fading influence by clinging to a man whose daily life mocks the very values that Christians seek to advance.

Mr. French in his article believes:

* The church is acting as if it needs Trump to protect it.
* That's not courageous. It's repulsive.
* If this fear continues, expect the church's witness to degrade further.
* In seeking protections from its perceived enemies, the church has lost its way.
* That America's conservative people of faith should seek a primary challenger to Trump.

Mr. French is a TIME columnist, a senior fellow at National Review, a Christian, a Presbyterian, an Iraq veteran, a graduate of the Harvard Law School, and a practicing attorney in Columbia, TN.

Mr. French quotes 2 Timothy 1:7 from the (KJV: *"For God hath not given us the spirit of fear; but of power, and of love, and of a sound mind."* This same verse appears in the (NIV) as *"For the Spirit God gave us does not make us timid, but gives us power, love and self-discipline."* The word *"fear"* is used in one version of the Bible and the word *"timid"* is used in the other. The use of either of these words is correct. Personally, I prefer the use of *"timid"* in this passage.

The use of the word *"fear"* is not appropriate in the life of any Christian whether they are classified as evangelicals, conservatives, liberals or lukewarm believers. Christians belong to Christ and are responsible to him for their lifestyles. The Scriptures are often misused and twisted to conform to a person's point of view.

Christians aren't to fear, but instead have *concerns* for the state of this nation. Every bad thing which happens in this country isn't caused by our sitting president nor caused by any candidate, regardless of party. We will continue forever to accuse former presidents for the events which happened under their administrations. People who commit acts of injustice toward others are the responsible ones. Neither are churches or Christians to be blamed. Christians are responsible only to God for their actions. And they are responsible to the governing authorities when civil laws are violated.

This article by Mr. French is what the media today is all about. The media is about brainwashing and selling their ideas, theories, beliefs, feelings and anything to make a profit. The liberal media preaches their agenda to the masses in their effort to influence others with their liberal, humanistic philosophies.

The church lost its way long before the one who is seated in the Oval Office came along. There are many influences affecting the church. Our present president is not one of these. Churches lost their influence years and years ago and have been on the decline for decades. The media is responsible to the public to print the truth and not mix in their own ideas as being the truth.

Mr. French, as a Christian, should be aware from the Holy Bible that God places in authority individuals of his choosing.

> Let everyone be subject to the governing authorities, for there is no authority except that which God has established. The authorities that exist have been established by God. Consequently, whoever rebels against the authority is rebelling against what God has instituted, and those who

so will bring judgment on themselves (Romans 13:1-2).

Christians are not living in *"fear."* They are aware of the One who is in control. Their concern is about the welfare of America and the future of their children, grandchildren and great grandchildren.

The reader might ask: "Why does the author subscribe to TIME magazine?" My answer: to understand more about what liberals are thinking and writing about.

Christians are not to follow a man, woman, preacher, minister or anyone except the Lord God. The 23rd Psalm as recorded in the (KJV) states:

> The Lord is my shepherd; I shall not want. He maketh me to lie down in green pastures: he leadeth me beside the still waters. He restoreth my soul: he leadeth me in the paths of righteousness for his name's sake. Yea, though I walk through the valley of the shadow of death, I will fear no evil: for thou art with me; thy rod and thy staff they comfort me. Thou preparest a table before in the presence of mine enemies: thou anointest my head with oil; my cup runneth over. Surely goodness and mercy shall follow me all the days of my life: and I will dwell in the house of the Lord forever.

This same Psalm states, "I will fear no evil." This should be the practice of every true Bible-believing Christian.

✢ NEWSPAPERS/ONLINE NEWS/ TV NEWS/TALK SHOWS

There are more newspapers and networks, especially in America, that are slanted to the left than to the right.

According to Business Insider, using information obtained from a Pew Research Center study, large newspapers with liberal audiences are the *New York Times*, *The Washington Post* and *USA Today*. Online news sources with liberal audience include Google News, CNN, Huffington Post and Buzzfeed. Television news sources with liberal audiences include the *Colbert Report* and *MSNBC*. Fox *News'* audience leans conservative, while CNN, *ABC*, *CBS* and *NBC* have audiences which lean left.

✣ A SATARICAL ESSAY OR FOR REAL

The following article appeared in a local newspaper, *"The Rocky Mount Telegram"* on October 27, 2019 under the heading, "TIME TO EXPOSE THE 'EVIL' OF CONSERVATIVE VALUES." The newspaper doesn't describe the writer of the article as a satirist and neither does the writer so identify. Some readers of the newspaper could be led to believe its contents. Whether this was a satirical essay or not, movements are underway in America with leanings toward socialism. (Weeks after this article was printed, the writer submitted another article to the newspaper saying it was meant to be an article of satire.) Obviously, it was.

I submit this article in its entirety, since it appeared in a "speak up" column by a local resident.

> "It is past time someone exposed the festering illness in our country known as the conservative movement and that conglomeration's evils so that everyone can see for themselves how it is endangering our wonderfully progressive socialist crusade which is finally beginning to take off with the marvelous slate of presidential candidates offered by the Democrats and with the election of the "Squad," our new mentors and thought police.

Just think about the conservatives' love of Christianity, that hateful religion that espouses a number of ridiculous ideas such as Jesus Christ died to absolve all of us, even Californians, of our sins; that marriage should be between a man and a woman; and that we should do unto others as we would have them do unto us. These religious nuts also came up with the equally offensive idea that there are only two genders and that it is biologically impossible to switch genders according to how you feel when you wake up in the morning. What insane beliefs!

These cretins also have this ridiculous philosophy that everyone is basically responsible for themselves and their families and that, with some obvious exceptions, everyone who is capable-of-working and earning a living should actually-have a job and strive to do so. They even believe that before a person is eligible to receive welfare or utilize Medicaid, that person should be investigated to determine whether they are capable-of-working and if they are, they should do so in order to be eligible. Insanity!

Further, they subscribe to the racist dogma that we should actually control our borders and not allow immigrants into our country until after they have properly applied for asylum and been vetted to the extent possible to assure they are not drug sellers, gang-bangers, wanted criminals, child molesters or other types of deviates and until they can show that they will be useful members of society and not a drain on the taxpayers They even want to build a horrible wall along the entire southern border to keep people from simply walking across as they have been doing for so many years. Cruelty personified!

Lastly, they actually-believe that the horrible Trump should be re-elected because we have such a great economy under his administration. They amazingly believe that the economy is more important than our precious identity politics. What completely demented folks!"

The majority of city and local community newspapers use the essays of liberal-leaning columnists on their editorial pages. One can determine whether their local newspaper is liberal or conservative by the number of liberal or conservative columnists which are printed on their editorial pages.

Rush Limbaugh is the most listened to radio talk show in America. He broadcasts on over 600 radio stations nationwide. In fun, he calls himself "America's Truth Detector." Sean Hannity, David Limbaugh (brother of Rush), Ann Coulter and Michael Savage are prominent conservatives.

Whether one sees, hears or reads local and national news, one doesn't know whether it's the truth or fiction. Newscasters comply to the leanings of their employers, whether liberal or conservative, reporting what they are told and how they are told to report it. Articles are scripted and edited in advance to express their liberal or conservative views.

The printing of religious articles, which were at one time prevalent in newspapers, are mostly a thing of the past. Newspapers which once included religious articles written by godly men and women are virtually a thing of the past. We are now living in a *"politically correct"* culture where primarily Christian messages are offensive to some. It should be obvious to Americans that no longer are they free to express vocal views and opinions. Americans are to have only one mindset - one that caters to the wishes of the minority.

The present-day strategy of movies, television programs, newspapers, magazines and advertisements are to promote every known liberal ungodly movement taking shape in these United States. And, there are many of these movements taking place in towns, cities and states. It is good fodder for their audiences.

CHAPTER THIRTY-FOUR

LESBIANS AND HOMOSEXUALS IN THE PULPITS

✛ THE LGBTQ MOVEMENT

THE LGBTQ MOVEMENT, WHICH INCLUDES LESBIANS, Gays, Bisexuals, and Transgenders, is widely publicized. The Q can mean either *"questioning" or "queer."* While some don't accept the addition of the letter *"Q,"* others do and say that a person can be all of the LGBTQ designations.

My first encounter with a gay person goes back to the year 1944 when I was sixteen years of age. In those days, gay men were referred to as *"queers."* In 1944, gays were not as visible. Multitudes were closeted.

The encounter occurred at the Crackers Baseball Park on Ponce de Leon Avenue, across from Sears, Roebuck & Company, in Atlanta. Sitting alone, I was joined by a friendly middle-aged male on the pretense of wanting to become my friend or a father figure.

We watched the game together, and afterwards he wanted to walk with me to the bus stop, which was about one-quarter of a mile away. He suggested that we take a little shortcut on another street which wasn't as crowded, and unknown to me, the streetlights were not as plentiful. Then, he made his play. I was having none of that. Feeling threatened and fearful by his insistence for sex, I agreed to meet him at a diner on Peachtree Street the next day. I had no intention of keeping the appointment.

The next morning, I told my stepfather about what had happened. He was furious, telling me that I would keep the appointment and that he was going with me.

My stepfather remained out of sight as I approached the diner. And, there he was, the gay man, smiling as he approached me. My stepfather came out of hiding, running and shouting toward the man. The man outran my stepfather down Peachtree Street, and I never saw him again. I never knew my stepfather's intentions. He was a volunteer deputy sheriff in the Atlanta area, and whether he intended to arrest the man for child abuse or do otherwise remains unknown to me.

My next encounters with gay individuals were in New York City's Times Square in 1947 and 1948. It was impossible for a solitary young man in uniform to walk peacefully at night in this area without being approached and accosted by those who were gay. They came out of their hiding places to prey on the young.

My last known encounter with a gay man back then was in the Soldiers and Sailors Club in New York City. He also wore a military uniform. He was insistent in his approach and almost threatening. Homosexuals were still in their closets in 1946 and 1947 and would remain there for some time.

✣ SEEKING LEADERSHIP WITHIN THE CHURCH

There are gays, lesbians, bisexuals, and I would suppose even transgenders in Christian churches throughout the world. Now, all sinners should be welcomed by Christian churches, but they should not be allowed or permitted to occupy Christian pulpits or to take-up teaching or places of leadership within the church. Why? The Bible, and Christian doctrine, prohibits it.

Yet, some denominations have and are considering permitting people with sexual issues to occupy places of leadership and allow them to conduct marriages for those of the same persuasion. Christian pastors should not preform same sex marriages.

One has only to look at the Roman Catholic Church to know that an unknown number of children have been abused by their priests and even those who hold other places of leadership. There are untold numbers of bishops, priests, and even cardinals within this faith, who have and who still are using their chosen profession to abuse the innocent.

An article, *"Group Denied Over LGBTQ Policy"* appeared in newspapers recently:

> "Duke University's student government has rejected a national Christian organization as an official student group because its policy excludes LGBTQ individuals from leadership positions. Last week, citing a rule every student group must include a nondiscrimination statement in the constitution to receive recognition and funding. Senators cited Young Life's sexual misconduct policy, which said it doesn't exclude people 'who practice a homosexual lifestyle from being recipients of ministry of God's grace,' however, they're 'not to serve as staff or volunteers.'
>
> Jeff Bennett, a member of the Duke chapter said it can't break national policies.
>
> Young Life's national spokesman Terry Swensen told The News & Observer that it's willing to help the chapter conform to Duke's rules."

The pulpits and other places of leadership are not for lesbians, gays, bisexuals, and transgenders in Christian churches. They cannot teach or practice the Bible for it is full of God's condemnation of homosexuality. Some defenders of the rights of gays will say that they can preach other teachings in which they believe. God's word is not a pick and choose book. Other defenders say that as Christians, we are to love them. It's not a case of loving them, but of hating their sin.

✢ SODOM AND GOMORRAH

What does the Lord God say about homosexuality?

Most people in Sodom and Gomorrah were so evil that the Lord God and two of his angels personally appeared before Abraham to discuss the situation. God's love for Abraham was so great that he wanted Abraham to know what was going to happen in these two places. Abraham had a nephew, Lot, and his family who lived in the area which God was planning to destroy.

Abraham began to plead with God about his destructive plan, for he loved his nephew. Then Abraham approached God and said:

> "Will you sweep away the righteous with the wicked? What if there are fifty righteous people in the city? Will you really sweep it away and not spare the place for the sake of the fifty righteous people in it? (Gen 18: 23-24)

Abraham, after a little thought, wanted to bargain somewhat with the Lord God:

> "What if the number of the righteous is five less than fifty? Will you destroy the whole city for the lack of five people?" "If I find forty-five there." God said. "I will not destroy it" (Gen 18: 27-28).

Abraham, in his boldness and questioning of God, moved to forty righteous, then thirty, next to twenty, and finally to only ten righteous. God made a promise to Abraham that if he found only ten righteous people in Sodom, the city would not be destroyed.

Here is what God had to say through the Apostle Paul in the New Testament about homosexuality:

> Because of this, God gave them over to shameful lusts. Even their women exchanged natural sexual relations for unnatural ones. In the same way the men also abandoned natural relations with women and were inflamed with lust for one another. Men committed shameful acts with other men, and received in themselves the due penalty for their error. Furthermore, just as they did not think it worthwhile to retain the knowledge of God, so God gave them over to a depraved mind, so that they do what ought not to be done. They have become filled with every kind of wickedness, evil, greed and depravity. They are full of envy, murder, strife, deceit and malice. They are gossips, slanderers, God-haters, insolent, arrogant, and boastful; they invent ways of doing evil; they disobey their parents; they have no understanding, no fidelity, no love, no mercy. Although they know God's righteous decree that those who do such things deserve death, they not only continue to do these very things but also approve of those who practice them (Romans 1: 26-32).

The Apostle Paul in a letter to the Church at Corinth writes:

> Or do you not know that wrongdoers will not inherit the kingdom of God? Do not be deceived: Neither the sexually immoral nor idolaters nor

adulterers nor men who have sex with men nor thieves nor the greedy nor drunkards nor slanderers nor swindlers will inherit the kingdom of God. And that is what some of you were. But you were washed, you were sanctified, you were justified in the name of the Lord Jesus Christ and by the Spirit of our God (1 Cor. 6: 9-11).

Will homosexuals go to Heaven? According to the previous passage written by the apostle, only those who have repented of their homosexuality, been washed, sanctified, and justified in the name of the Lord Jesus Christ and by the Spirit of God.

I have been acquainted with only one repentant homosexual during my Christian ministry. He is now living a Christian lifestyle.

✛ PROMOTING THE MOVEMENT

On the cover of *Time* magazine on May 13, 2019 appeared the picture of two practicing homosexuals. One of these two men announced that he is running for the office of the president of the United States of America. The cover page had the caption *"First Family."* The hopeful is Pete Buttigieg, former mayor of South Bend, who presently is also in the role of being a *"wife"* to *his* *"husband"* who is also pictured in this gay relationship. *Time* writes that Mr. Buttigieg is a veteran, a Christian and the first openly gay man to make a serious bid for president.

Someone may now ask, "Is Mr. Buttigieg a Christian or not a Christian?" My only answer is this: According to the Holy Bible of God, he isn't a Christian.

Should former mayor Buttigieg become the President of the United States of America, newspapers and magazines throughout the USA should read? *"THE NEW SODOM AND GOMARRAH: THE UNITED STATES OF AMERICA."* Will they?

The breakfast cereal, "Cheerios," pictures Ellen DeGeneres on boxes which go into the home of millions of Americans each day. Ms. DeGeneres is a very funny and well-known comedian but should not be a role model for America's young people.

Some will ask if Christians hate homosexuals. No! They hate the sin. The God of the Bible does not teach Christians to hate, but to love those who are caught up in sinful lifestyles.

Can LGBTQ people become and are members of churches? Absolutely! But not a part of the clergy.

People ask today, why does the Lord God put up with what is happening in our world where there is so much wickedness? My answer is that God is still finding at least ten righteous people among us.

✢ GAY FAMILY MEMBERS

If some of your family members are like some of mine, then you have family members who are gay. I still love them, pray for them and continue to hate the sin in which they are engaged.

Recently during television's *Wheel of Fortune,* a male participant said that his husband in the audience would not be happy with him if he risked his present winnings and justified his decision by saying that they were planning soon to adopt children. And on *Jeopardy* after the first commercial break, a male participant announced that his husband was in the audience. The LGBTQ movement is becoming more vocal and publicized.

The LGBTQ movement spends millions of dollars to promote their cause. It is also being promoted at no charge in living rooms throughout America by newspapers, television, movies, social media, industry, celebrities, and a host of actors, whether in Hollywood or elsewhere. Some have come out of the closet, while others remain hidden behind closed doors.

✣ HIGH GOVERNMENT OFFICIALS

On January 3, 2019, the 116th Congress of the United States was sworn in. There are now ten members who are openly lesbians, gays, or bisexuals. Eight are in the House and two are in the Senate. All of them are Democrats.

Many folks are of the opinion that lesbians, gays, bisexuals, and transgenders were made to be that way by God. Therefore, they reason that if God made them that way there is no way that they are to be blamed or criticized for their actions. Therefore, God is the one to be blamed. The God I know from the Bible doesn't lead anyone into sinful actions or deeds.

Being gay is solely by choice. I couldn't be more emphatic about "by choice." Sexual orientation is a choice made by the individual. God creates people by sex, male and female. It shouldn't be difficult for anyone to identify their sex on an application or on any other sheet of paper.

Some make claims that they don't know whether they are male or female. Therefore, choices on forms are expanded beyond male and female.

✣ FRICTION WITHIN DENOMINATIONS

Christians should be concerned about the LGBTQ's infiltration within Christian denominations seeking to fill pulpits and the marriage of people of the same sex. There's a growing range of political and cultural activism in some parts of the world which includes lobbying, street marches, social groups, media, art and research. Untold millions of dollars are being spent to promote LGBTQ.

According to Pew research, denominations which are now performing same sex marriages include the United Church of Christ, Metropolitan Community Church, The Reform and Conservative Jewish Movements and The Unitarian Universalist Association. The Presbyterian Church (U.S.A.) and the Episcopal Church recently voted to perform same sex marriages.

Some churches which are NOT performing same sex marriages are: The Roman Catholic Church, The Orthodox Jewish Movement, The Southern Baptist Convention, the National Baptist Convention and the Assemblies of God.

The United Methodist Church has been debating the issue of same sex marriages and it is getting more difficult for them to maintain unity. Some UMC clergy are performing same sex marriages. On a much smaller scale, some Southern Baptist clergy have done so as well.

The Church of Jesus Christ of Latter-day Saints, which is not considered to be Christian, but a cult, does not perform same sex marriages.

According to the *Christian Post*, "The Reformed Church in America is another reformed denomination in the USA with gay clergy serving congregations. Their ordination is from other denominations."

The United Church of Christ; The Evangelical Lutheran Church in America; and the Episcopal Church, already allow the ordination of openly gay candidates. The Presbyterian church (U.S.A.) has become the fourth Protestant denomination to allow the ordination of gay and lesbian clergy.

In the future, the LGBTQ movement will continue to become larger and more demanding with its blending practices. That is why some of the pages of this book is devoted to giving the reader a glimpse into how homosexuality is playing a part in the decline of Christian churches here in the United States.

CHAPTER THIRTY-FIVE

RACISM

✦ MORE ABOUT ME

MY ROOTS STARTED IN A LITTLE TOWN IN SOUTH Georgia many moons ago. My mother, after her divorce, moved back home with her parents in a little town, which claimed only one caution light on Highway 41. This road was the main thoroughfare from Atlanta to the sunshine state of Florida. The population was minute and included white and black folks.

My grandfather, an entrepreneur, operated a meat market. Coca Cola was a nickel so was a hamburger. These were the 1930s. There weren't any health certificates needed for his store nor were there any restrictions or inspections for butchering his meat from an oak tree in the front yard.

He was a great gardener. With a mule and a plow, he planted a garden each year, growing more vegetables than needed for our family. The harvest from the garden brought me to my first experience with the people-of-color in town.

My grandmother loved sitting on the front porch of her little wood-frame house which rested about a half mile off Highway 41. Houses there didn't have garages or carports. People in this small town couldn't afford automobiles.

One day a black woman stopped to ask if she could buy a mess of collards for her evening meal. With my grandmother's nod of affirmation, the woman of color asked, *"How much?"* *"A nickel,"* answered my grandma. *"Go and pick all that you need."*

My grandparents had never discussed with us why some folks were black and why we were white. If there were racism present, it wasn't visible or mentioned.

My mother remarried and we pulled up stakes and moved to Atlanta. In the city limits of Atlanta, there were four high schools for the whites. The Booker T. Washington school in Atlanta was constructed in 1924 and was the only secondary school for blacks until 1947. Blacks were not allowed admission to the white schools.

The city schools didn't have buses to transport school children from their homes to these white schools. A nickel token was charged each way for city transportation. Whites were seated from the front to the rear of the bus and blacks were to sit from the back to the front.

In the neighborhoods on the southeast side of Atlanta, we rented a wood-framed duplex. There was a large community of black folks which was called *"Smith's Bottom"* living in the rear of the duplex. They walked the paved sidewalks in the neighborhood the same as white folks but were not allowed to live among the whites up on the streets.

The only openly racist that was in my family was an uncle who was married to one of my mother's sisters. He was belligerent in his demands for a black person to go to the back door should they knock at the front door.

During my boot camp days in 1946, there were two black seamen who were quartered in the same barracks. There was a racial problem on one occasion, and it was provoked by a white seaman. The two of them, one white and one black went outside to settle their differences. After that instance, there wasn't a conflict.

On our first leave in 1946, a military bus took our group into Jacksonville, FL for a weekend. Along the way, the two black seamen were dropped off in the black section of the city. They had gone through the same routines which we all had experienced together but were not permitted to enter into the white area.

At the age of 18, after boot training, I was stationed in Washington, DC, where I worked among many black civil service employees. Some of them had racist attitudes. Some kidded me about being from the South and asked if my family were members of the KKK. Their comments appeared to be racist, but I considered them as being more directed to the South in general rather than to me.

✦ BLACK AND WHITE TOGETHERNESS

Recently, I attended a two-day affair where one predominately white congregation and a predominately black church had a couple of sessions together. Wow! The Spirit of God permeated the meetings.

At first it appeared that both the whites and the blacks wanted to spread out among the sanctuary and to sit apart from each other. The minister of the black constituents noticed that as well. He asked that the salt and the pepper get closer together by saying, "Eggs always need a little black and white seasoning to make them taste better."

These two meetings were great but only temporary. What was done later? The whites and people of color went back to where they were before the meetings.

I recall another example of racism. A potential white applicant for a staff position at a large Protestant church brought along some black folks for a dinner meeting. Later, a church member thinking that the candidate would be employed, remarked, "I guess that will be the way it will be in OUR church."

Christians should know and realize that 'OUR church' is 'NOT OUR church.' The church is GOD's church.

A few months after the arrival of a new pastor in a community where the congregation was 99.9% white, but the community to be served was predominately saturated with black people, I said to him, "All you have to do is to look at the congregation to see that we haven't been doing our job."

I have been fellowshipping with, teaching to and preaching to black folks for years. When I feel spiritually undernourished, I will visit a black church to get fed some spiritual or "soul" food. In some of these churches which I have visited, there isn't a concern for starting on time and ending on time. There were warm and sincere greetings. When it comes to worshipping the Lord, what you feel is what you get.

On one occasion in a black church, the minister insisted that I speak to the people. The reason for his asking, I surmise, was to see if I had a word from the Lord which could uplift his people. In this church, the way in which they were worshipping the Lord God was totally different and more spiritual from what I have felt in some white congregations. There wasn't any rolling in the aisles nor was there any talking in unknown tongues. The people came to do what they had come to do - to worship the King.

Personally, some black folks wouldn't be happy in worshipping in white folks' churches. And, white folks wouldn't be happy worshipping the way that black folks worship. This statement has overtones of racism and has probably been used before to justify the separation of the races.

Before Lyndon B. Johnson passed the Civil Rights Act in 1964, I was pastoring a church in Washington state. One of the ladies in the church asked me to visit a jail with her and to do a devotion with some women prostitutes. The cellblock was full of whites and blacks. The devotion was well received.

Within a period of two to three weeks after the visit to the jail, one of the black prostitutes was released and on a Wednesday night, came to a prayer meeting. Some within the membership wanted to know who she was. To my knowledge, she was the first black having ever attended there at the church. I was later asked by one of the deacons if I really needed to participate in any other meetings at the jail. I didn't ask why or even give a reply to his question, figuring that it was probably motivated by racialism, and not by the fact that the woman was a prostitute.

✢ RACISM STILL FOR REAL

In recent years, while doing an interim pastorship in a North Carolina church, there was a lady who was adamant in her desire for the church to stay white. However, she brought with her each Sunday caregivers who were black.

There was no doubt about this woman's Christianity. She had attended this church her entire life, and white is what it had always been. She wanted it to stay that way. After her death, the church closed its doors due to declining membership. Instead of a church setting on a corner in a small town preaching the Gospel of Jesus Christ, it now has become a dilapidated building "which has gone out of business."

✢ DENIALS BY EVERYONE

All of us, to some extent, are racist. That includes black people as well as white folks. I have lived in the South most of my life. Also, I have lived a few years in the North and Northwest. I have been acquainted with both black and white racists in all these areas.

Of course, denials of our racism come after some of our racist comments.

"I'm not racist, but..." I have heard that statement so many times. Tongues say different things than what the heart is feeling. When it comes to racism, many lies and justifications are spoken, and not the truth.

Do I think in my lifetime that most whites will be totally comfortable in churches which are primarily black? No!

Do I think in my lifetime that most blacks will be totally comfortable in churches which are primarily white? No!

The only "yes" that I could give these two questions would be in the giant mega-churches where the average attendance each Sunday is in excess of thousands. These thousands in mega-churches are there for a very short period and are not involved in the everyday activities of the church.

Thousands of black and white folks go to football and basketball stadiums to cheer on their teams. They get along together for this brief period-of-time, motivated by the love for their teams. If you want a beer, a hot dog, or a hamburger, there are no problems in rubbing elbows with each other. No reasons exist to remain together after the game. There aren't any by-laws or committee meetings. These blacks and whites are together for a temporary event. They do not have to work together afterwards to make decisions. And after attending a ballgame, each goes their own way.

Will there ever be an end to racism? No! It's becoming more relevant both to blacks and whites. There are many groups among whites and blacks that promote racism. Instead of blacks and whites moving ahead in harmony, headlines and daily events announce that we are going backward instead of forward.

There is racism on each side of the divide which is cheered on and encouraged by the media. The media will always be looking for news - even if they go back for generations and decades to fan the flames. Any flicker of racism, and more newspapers, magazines and television ads get sold.

✢ POLITICS AND RACISM

The latest in recent newsprint is the situation with the governor of Virginia who is having difficulty remembering whether he is in "blackface" or in a "KKK outfit" in one of his yearbooks while in medical school. One day he admits that he is in the pictures, and the next day he's not. I do not think so. To be in such an executive position as the governor of Virginia, he has a rather short, convenient memory.

I wonder if Asa Yoelson (Al Jolson) was a racist to the millions that went to his performances. He owned Broadway in New York City for many years and later went to Hollywood and made movies. Some black publications praised him while some white publications were critical of him.

Racism will always be an issue in America. It's ignited by the media and networks daily. Some people are reliving the past to promote racism.

I can never realize what it's like to be a person of color, having never walked in a black person's shoes. I, too, have been discriminated against and have felt like a person living in an alien society, but not like a black person. My discrimination wasn't racism. I have experienced only a touch of what it feels like when a person is made to feel like the lowest person on a totem pole. My feelings are minute in comparison to what black people have experienced.

A consolation statement made to a person who is undergoing a traumatic experience, ("I know how you feel.") is not possibly accurate unless you have been through the same experience. One must go through a similar experience to understand the pain. White and black Christians will never bury racism. Past circumstances and history can and will not ever be buried and forgotten. And neither can a person erase history.

CHAPTER THIRTY-SIX

TWO ORDINANCES

✢ BAPTISMS

HOW MANY BAPTISMS IN THE PAST FIVE YEARS WERE performed in the church which you now attend? Were these baptisms for children twelve years and younger or were they for adults, especially those of college age or older?

Since I am a member of a Baptist church which is associated with the Southern Baptist Convention, most of my research about these two ordinances come from SBC teachings.

First, to baptize according to Baptist belief or doctrine is to "plunge" or "immerse" someone like dyeing a piece of cloth. This is immersing or burying the entire body in water.

I have witnessed several prison inmates being baptized or immersed in water in portable baptismal pools. In these small portable pools, there is much splashing of water from the pool. With each baptism, there is less and less water. Some of the men whose bodies were not completely covered were baptized for a second time when more water was added to the portable. The entire body is given in totality to God.

The act of sprinkling the head as some denominational churches do, is not considered to be scriptural by Baptist churches. There are many different types of Baptists churches.

John the Baptist 'immersed' the Lord Jesus in the Jordan River.

"As soon as Jesus was baptized, he went up out of the water" (Matt. 3: 16a). Jesus' entire body was placed below the waters of the Jordan River near the town of Bethany.

Another passage from Scripture about baptismal immersing is when Philip, an evangelist, witnessed to the Ethiopian who was on his way home after worshipping in Jerusalem. The Ethiopian eunuch was reading from a scroll of Isaiah the prophet. The Spirit of God sent Philip to help the eunuch understand what he was reading. Philip was invited into the chariot by the Ethiopian. After achieving an understanding of the words of Isaiah, the Ethiopian said to Philip,

> "Look, here is water. What can stand in the way of my being baptized?" And he gave orders to stop the chariot. Then both Philip and the eunuch went down into the water and Philip baptized him (Acts 8: 36b-38).

✢ BAPTISM FOR THE CHRISTIAN

The Apostle Paul gives a reason for a Christian to be baptized.

> "Or don't you know that all of us who were baptized into Christ Jesus were baptized into his death? We were therefore buried with him through baptism into death in order that, just as Christ was raised from the dead through the glory of the Father, we too may live a new life" (Rom. 6: 3-4).

A Baptist church is a body of baptized believers, not sprinkled, but buried beneath the water and then raised to walk in newness of life.

Are you experiencing any water baptism in your church? The Southern Baptist Convention was once an evangelistic organization. Its major theme was to make disciples. The Great Commission was its primary goal. This should be the focus for all denominations. Today, less attention is given to making disciples. The focus today appears to be more on the maintenance of what a church has already attained.

✣ BAPTISMS WITHIN BAPTIST CHURCHES AND OTHER DENOMINATIONS

When I was associate pastor at Riverside Baptist Church in California, a family of five presented themselves for membership in a Sunday morning service. This family was coming by letters from another Baptist church. The senior pastor questioned their baptism by asking them if they had been baptized by immersion. By their admission they had not received baptism by immersion. Pastor Polk baptized them in the church's baptismal pool a week later.

Baptisms does not have a saving effect. It is one of two ordinances commanded by the Lord Jesus. Saved persons go into the baptismal pool after being washed in the blood of Christ Jesus. Many people are baptized having never repented of their sins and not having had a personal relationship with our Lord. These go into the baptismal waters a dry sinner and come up out of the water a wet sinner.

Some denominational churches teach that baptism is part of the saving process. That isn't Scriptural. What Jesus did on Calvary's cross is sufficient.

During the first century, some Hebrews taught that you had to be circumcised in order to receive salvation. The Jerusalem church put an end to that teaching according to Acts 15.

Many soldiers, sailors, marines, and airmen, whether in fox holes, sinking ships, etc., have made professions of faith and were saved when baptism was not possible at the time. God doesn't need anything added to the shedding of his Son's blood.

Church members, for their own personal reasons, move from one denomination to another caused by disenchantments, mobility or likes and dislikes. Several denominations sprinkle instead of immersing. When I was an associate in a Methodist Church, a person could choose to be sprinkled or immersed. Most members chose the sprinkling process because it was more convenient.

Methodist churches don't have baptismal pools, but a body of water may easily be found for those who want to be immersed like Jesus. When those who have been sprinkled within other denominations come for membership, Baptists require that these persons be taken into the baptismal waters to be immersed.

Some denominations or groups point out that all New Testament baptisms occurred outside in running water. They say nothing else counts.

Some ministers within Baptist churches don't ask or check to see how a person was baptized when coming from another denomination. It's surprising (though I don't know why) that persons coming from another Baptist congregation are not asked about their baptism. The world is so mobile that a person could have been in several denominations before reaching their present church without scriptural baptism being administered.

✢ ONE BAPTISM OR TWO

Last year I went to a baptismal service where a husband and wife were baptized for the second time. As youths they had joined the church by profession of their faith in Christ Jesus but were not sincere. Their previous decisions to join the church when younger, were provoked by family members. Should records kept of those getting the cart before the horse decisions become known, it would be startling. The couple's names were already listed on the church's membership rolls, therefore, there were no new members. Were their names again reported to the convention's roll as baptisms and new members? You can count on it. It's impossible to maintain accurate statistics.

In years of working within the walls of jails and prisons, I have been acquainted with many men who confessed to their getting-the-cart-before-the-horse decisions. Within one prison in North Carolina, it's estimated that over half of the sixty plus men baptized within a two-year period were men who were being rebaptized and had gotten the cart before the horse.

Some of these incarcerated men were hostile, discouraged and disappointed about their prior experience within former churches. It's easy to point fingers or put the blame elsewhere, but I don't feel that was what they were doing. Their criticisms were directed toward the hypocrisy of former church members and some of their former pastors.

✢ Baptism is Required of New Converts

Some baptismal pools are never used. Little emphasis and evangelistic efforts are being placed on baptisms by some congregations. Since there are few baptisms or no baptisms, emphasis is placed somewhere else. Without evangelism in a church or the public witnessing of its members, the lost cannot be led to Christ.

Any organization, whether Christian or not, will not remain in business without growth. This is one of the reasons for the decline of the church. The lost are not being reached. The hunger for lost souls is no longer primary.

✝ HOLY COMMUNION/LORD'S SUPPER

The observance of Holy Communion is Jesus' second ordinance which is to be carried out by the church. Some churches use the term "The Lord's Supper." Many Protestant churches have a table located by the pulpit with the carved words "DO THIS IN REMEMBRANCE OF ME."

Jesus initiated this ordinance when he had the Passover meal with his disciples before being arrested on the Mount of Olives.

> While they were eating, Jesus took bread, and when he had given thanks, he broke it and gave it to his disciples, saying, "Take and eat; this is my body." Then he took a cup, and when he had given thanks, he gave it to them, saying, "Drink from it, all of you. This is my blood of the covenant, which is poured out for many for the forgiveness of sins. I tell you, I will not drink from this fruit of the vine from now on until that day when I drink it new with you in my Father's kingdom." When they had sung a hymn, they went out to the Mount of Olives (Matthew 26: 26-30).

The Bible does not say how often the Lord's Supper is to be observed by the church. When and how often is determined by the pastor, deacons or elders of a church. Denominational churches will observe it weekly, monthly or quarterly. Some churches tack it on at the conclusion of a service and with very little, if any, reverence.

Some churches use the fermented fruit of the vine (wine) while other churches use unfermented grape juice. Holy

Communion is observed, depending on the church, in several ways. The juice may be served in one cup or individual cups. Churches may use one huge piece of unleavened bread or flakes of unleavened bread.

When God's Word doesn't give implicit instructions, it becomes necessary to ask in prayer what is His direction. One can get very close to God when observing Holy Communion if one's mind is not on a roast cooking in the oven at home or getting to the cafeteria before other churches arrive.

The Lord's Supper in the first century was being abused by the way it was observed in the church at Corinth. The apostle Paul, in detail, explained its meaning and how it was to be conducted.

> So then; when you come together, it is not the Lord's Supper you eat, for when you are eating, some of you go ahead with your own private suppers. As a result, one person remains hungry and another gets drunk. Don't you have homes to eat and drink in? Or do you despise the church of God by humiliating those who have nothing? What shall I say to you? Shall I praise you? Certainly not in this matter! (1 Cor 11: 20-22).

Paul is probably not talking about how it was to be conducted, but how it was being abused. Paul, in his corrective manner, and under the inspiration of the Holy Spirit, explained that what these church members were doing was a practice which was not in keeping with the intent initiated by the Lord. First, it had turned into a social gathering. Secondly, the Lord Supper was being used as an occasion to get drunk. Thirdly, there were those who didn't have food to bring. Fourthly, there was the lack of a spiritual element. Fifthly, some were setting themselves apart from others. The Lord wasn't to be remembered in this way.

This, Paul says, is the proper way to have this ordinance:

For I received from the Lord what I also passed on to you: The Lord Jesus, on the night he was betrayed, took bread, and when he had given thanks, he broke it and said, "This is my body, which is for you; do this in remembrance of me." In the same way, after supper he took the cup, saying, "This cup is the new covenant in my blood; do this, whenever you drink it, in remembrance of me." For whenever you eat this bread and drink this cup, you proclaim the Lord's death until he comes.

So then, whoever eats the bread or drinks the cup of the Lord in an unworthy manner will be guilty of sinning against the body and blood of the Lord. Everyone ought to examine themselves' before they eat of the bread and drink from the cup. For those who eat and drink without discerning the body of Christ eat and drink judgment on themselves (1 Cor. 11:27-29).

Regardless of how some church members observe, believe or feel about the Lord's Supper, being a participant in it is a serious matter. It is not to be taken lightly or tacked on at the end of a worship service. Only those who are Christians are to participate in the Lord's Supper. Some parents will permit their children, who aren't members, to participate. It has no meaning for an unbeliever.

Some churches exercise what is called "closed" communion. Those churches practicing this policy will permit only their members to participate. Other churches will invite Christians from all denominations to the table of the Lord.

Jesus commanded his disciples to engage in these two ordinances until He returns. His return will be His second coming. "Do this in remembrance of me."

Less is being done by many denominations to spiritually engage in these two ordinances. Today's Christians continue to move away from the teaching of the Shepherd.

CHAPTER THIRTY-SEVEN

THE CHURCH WITHIN THE COMMUNITY

✚ CHURCHES IN DOWNTOWN AREAS

THE CHURCH IN ANY COMMUNITY IS THERE FOR ONE primary purpose - to reach the lost by making disciples. Statistics reveal that this isn't being done.

Some downtown churches, chartered a hundred years ago or more, remain in their downtown locations in many towns and cities across America. These can be noted by the designation of having in the name of their title, the word 'First.' This is true in most instances.

Most rural and suburban churches usually are smaller in size. These churches vary in sizes: large to small, living room, storefront or with a campus and some with graveyards.

There are various reasons why these large downtown churches remain downtown. Historically, when blacks move into a neighborhood, whites move out to the suburbs. Churches in downtown areas where businesses remain, white members will stay in their large expensive buildings of stone, brick and mortar. Usually, there isn't an effort on the part of white members to reach out to the black community.

White members will travel on Sundays from their suburban homes to worship in the buildings in which their ancestors worshipped. Whether downtown churches move or stay, the emphasis should remain to reach the community regardless of the races. Integration isn't on the front burner. Integration isn't welcomed.

There are movements now among some white churches with programs to reach out to both the black and the white school children. These programs are held after the school day is over for a few days each week.

There are other activities within churches to dispatch vans and school buses to transport children on Sunday for the Bible study hour. These efforts are meant to reach adults through their children.

These programs are a true evangelistic effort on the part of some to reach the lost in the community. Evangelism is dead in many churches, since there isn't a true hunger in the hearts of the elderly membership to reach those who are lost. Many of these "First" churches in downtown areas are interested in maintaining their status quo. They want to keep the building open because that is where their Christianity began.

It should be asked: "What is the church which I am attending doing to reach those in *the* shadows of the church?" Many believers, and especially unbelievers within the confines of the church are of the opinion that they don't know how to witness even though they are witnessing every day by their lifestyles and their deeds. The ways Christians live are reflections of their beliefs. The lifestyles of Christians should be different from the lifestyles of those who are lost.

After a church service one Sunday morning in Washington state, a member asked if I would come to his home that afternoon to help lead to Christ a relative who was visiting him. He didn't know how to do it himself.

When someone walks the aisles after a preaching service and wants to accept Christ as their Savior, a time of rejoicing should occur by the membership. The Holy Spirit has already begun His work by bringing conviction and repentance to the heart of that person before a person walks the aisles. Some pastors might treat a profession of faith lightly. For the one coming forward to publicly acknowledge Christ as His savior, it's the most important decision which he will ever make. It's the church's responsibility to take a new convert under its wings and ask a member to personally help the new Christian to grow in his faith. A person just coming to the faith should not be left alone to ponder and grow.

God has placed and planted your church in an area for the sole purpose of reaching that community. A church will know how effective their ministry is in the community when they see people walking the aisles.

✢ RURAL CHURCHES

Rural churches are closing their doors faster than the more organized and programmed larger churches in downtown areas. The rural churches are those saturated with several family members. Everyone is acquainted with each other and usually will know most everything about each other. It's a close-knit living community where members spend even more time together when away from the church. Peer pressure is more prevalent. Some of these churches will maintain cemeteries for their departed members.

Sons and daughters of these rural churches grew up together, joined the church together, and went to colleges and universities together. After graduation, their careers were begun in other areas having more opportunities. They started their families and never returned home. The grandpas and grandmas would soon go to be with the Lord, leaving their parents and their neighbors in a church with less children and an uncertain future. These churches, when failing to attract and reach out to their community, will soon close their doors. Some have already begun to die an earlier death when some families left the church for downtown or suburban churches where programs for their children were offered.

Within the last five years, I have served as interim or supply pastor at two churches where their doors are now closed. These two buildings remain empty and idle. A cemetery, behind one of these churches, shows some maintenance activity at times.

There is another church, just two blocks from where I am writing this book which closed its doors three years ago. The building was bought by another Baptist church for a mission to Spanish speaking people. The church's building remains a symbol for the Lord.

✟ SUBURBAN CHURCHES IN POPULATED AREAS

These churches have many similarities of the rural church. However, some were started in homes in developing suburban neighborhoods where whites fled to escape the integration of their neighborhoods in downtown areas.

Some already established suburban churches gladly opened their doors to these former members of downtown churches. New malls, new schools, new jobs, new homes, new neighbors and new surroundings awaited. Veterans returned from World War II and the Korean War, and homes were being purchased under the GI Bill of Rights.

The same routines of church members from downtown churches were brought with them to their new church in the suburbs. What they had been doing in their downtown church remained the same. Without renewed delicateness on the part of the transferee, the same mode of operation present in the old environment continued.

✣ THE BAGS OF GOLD/TALENTS

> "Again, it will be like a man going on a journey, who called his servants and entrusted his wealth to them. To one he gave five bags of gold, to another two bags, and to another one bag, each according to his ability. Then he went on his journey. The man who had received five bags of gold went at once and put his money to work and gained five bags more. So also, the one with two bags of gold gained two more. But the man who had received one bag went off, dug a hole in the ground and hid his master's money" (Matt. 25: 14-18).

Jesus was instructing his disciples about using the talents which were given to them. He would be leaving them soon, but they would not be alone. Jesus would give talents to each disciple, according to their abilities. To some of them he would give more and to others he would give less. He would be expecting each of them to use these talents for the work of His kingdom.

Two of these disciples immediately went to work and doubled them. The one receiving the one talent went and dug a hole and buried it in the ground.

This is what is happening in the today's churches, whether in downtown, rural or suburban areas. The talents given by God to his chosen and converted are not being used. It's not that disciples no longer have these talents. Church members have dug holes, expecting someone else to do their work.

In our culture we pay others to do work which we don't want to do. We can't pay someone to do God's work for us. Some paid employees would also like to do what we are doing - nothing. Hired help don't have God-given talents to do His work.

It is reasonable to assume that many who moved to the suburbs from the downtown areas were not members of churches and were not Christians. The existing churches in the suburbs had a blooming harvest field - ripe and ready for the picking. Some within these existing suburban churches were comfortable with their present circumstances and were unwilling to change or to venture out with the challenge to reach their neighborhood.

Some question why churches just around the corner from other churches are growing while others are not. God has already left some churches.

CHAPTER THIRTY-EIGHT

CHRISTIAN LIFESTYLES

TRUE LIFE STORIES: (Names have been changed to protect their identity)

✤ "MARY JANE"

A MARRIED WOMAN, WELL RESPECTED AND FORTYISH, was a devoted church goer when she was in town and not traveling in her profession. She loved the outdoors. Her husband was not the best dresser and often looked as if he was coming from a chore in the yard when he attended church with her on Sundays.

Phil, her husband, was professional, college educated, and very respected in his role as an attorney. Outside of their attendance at church, the two of them were seldom ever seen together. They had been in a martial relationship for years.

Mary Jane's eyes began to focus on and take an interest in Joe, an entrepreneur, also married, who had recently moved to town, and now attending the same church which she attended. From all indication, Joe was not aware of Mary's interest in him.

The two families had been seen together at a few local events, but these events were very rare.

Mary Jane began going by Joe's business wanting to discuss the Bible. There were many occasions where the discussions ended outside on the street as Joe would walk Mary Jane back to her car. Outside the walls of the business and the hearing of others, these discussions would last fifteen to twenty minutes.

Joe's wife, Kate, who worked at the business, began noticing Mary's attraction to her husband. Kate confronted Joe, put her foot down by saying there will be no more of these come by visits by Mary Jane. Joe denied any guilt and told Kate that she was wrong with her analysis of Mary Jane's intentions. Kate's intuition was right on target. Mary Jane would have to find another attraction. *"The nipping of the bud"* became effective before any further romantic interest cultivated.

After Kate's confrontation with Joe, there weren't any more visits by Mary Jane.

✢ "VIVIAN"

She was a churchgoing woman who had been taught to go to church on Sundays. Her father was a devout Christian who took pride in having two daughters whom he doted on. His Saturday routine was to take his two girls to their small town and treat them as queens. He was a devoted family man, a hard worker and a successful businessman.

Juanita, the older of the two daughters, married, had two children and spent her entire life loving her husband and two children.

Vivian was more adventure prone. She married right after high school, but the marriage didn't last. After the divorce, her father sent Vivian off to college where she obtained a master's degree. She remarried soon after graduation and bore a son. This marriage was also a short and rocky one.

After her father died, Vivian was now on her own and had to support a son. Vivian was not meant to live alone. The two previous marriages weren't happy ones, and there wasn't a

Daddy now to help her with the rearing of her son. Her father had spoiled her.

Vivian didn't like to work and didn't have to when her father was alive. Because of circumstances now - found employment.

Vivian's focus soon rested on a coworker who was married and making an income far greater than hers. Her flirtations began. Paul had been married for several years and had a son when Paul was in his early twenties. According to Paul, there had never been discontent or unhappiness in his marriage.

Vivian, although a church going woman, had no qualms about breaking up a marriage. Her father had always given her what she wanted. Why the two other marriages had early endings is unknown.

Within a year, Paul left his wife and married Vivian. Paul and Vivian claimed undying love for each other, but Vivian wanted more than her husband could give her. It appeared that she preferred her old lifestyle. There had been several men in her life, and she had more than one during this marriage. She loved variety.

Paul's jealousy and suspicion caused him to believe that his wife of a few years was now seeing some former men friends. Vivian vehemently denied any such accusations or claims by Paul.

A few years into their marriage, Paul's jealousy and beliefs caused him to investigate his suspicions. He found the one whom he believed was the one who truly loved him in a motel with another man.

✞ "BO'SEN"

A short term for Boatswain or a petty officer in the naval forces of the United States or the merchant marines.

The seamen under Bo'sen often called him *"Boats."* Bo'sen was a highly decorated Coast Guardsman, having won the

Silver Star and other medals for his bravery in the Pacific by putting infantry and vehicles ashore on islands held by the Japanese.

Bo'sen was a petty officer first class but was promoted for one day to the rank of Chief Petty Officer in order to participate in a highly publicized event. After the war in the Pacific, the Coast Guard sent him off to Washington, DC to chauffeur around some of the high brass.

Bo'sen was very highly respected by the seamen under him. He was loved by all. His heroism hadn't gone to his head, and he would get drunk and party with anyone who wanted to come along.

He was a churchgoing man. He and his wife never missed going to church on Sunday. One would never have known that Bo'sen was a godly man because of the way he lived his life during the week. He could swear and drink with the best of them. He lived the lifestyle of those who are without Christ.

✢ Your Thoughts

There are millions of similar stories in America.

Which of these three church members were Christians?

There isn't really a need to answer the question. All of them were Christians according to today's standards of having names on a church roll. Churchgoing has never made a person a Christian.

When you suffer from physical pain, you seek out a doctor or enter a hospital for treatment. The question is often asked of the hurting, "On a scale of one to ten, what is the level of your pain?"

If you are asking for a pain pill or some medication to alleviate the pain, your response should be a "five level or above," or you won't get the pain pill. When you are a Christian, your pain and guilt from sins will be relieved from the old desires and sins of your former way of living. It's painful when you are truly a Christian and are living in sin. There isn't any joy or peace within your soul. There isn't any happiness. You will know if you are living in God's will when joy and the peace of forgiveness permeate your life.

"Thou shalt not kill" has no meaning to some when choosing an abortion as an alternative. Abortions among churchgoing people are rampant. A life begins at conception. Statistics indicate that 37 out of 100 churchgoing women have had abortions. This is more than alarming when stated this way: 37 million churchgoing women out of 100 million have had abortions. Our bodies belong to God. He is the Creator of all life. No person has the authority to take the innocent life of another. Not even our own life.

Decades ago, a relative, as a young girl, became pregnant out of wedlock. She was living in a small town and everyone knew the business of others. It would become the gossip of the town if others knew of her being pregnant.

The father of the baby came from a prominent family and there wouldn't be a wedding. The family members of the young girl were churchgoers. There wouldn't be an abortion. Not only were they illegal at that time but they went against their biblical beliefs.

The decision was made to send the daughter and the girl's mother to live with a relative in a distant town until the baby was born. Returning to her home after the pregnancy, the mother of the girl claimed to be the mother of the child. The truth was never known until decades later when the woman who gave birth confessed to her children and grandchildren that she was not their aunt, but their mother and grandmother.

Today's culture is totally different from that of bygone years. The behavior and lifestyles of churchgoers are playing a major part in **THE KILLING OF THE CHRISTIAN CHURCH IN AMERICA.**

CHAPTER THIRTY-NINE

A SURVEY OF BIBLICAL KNOWLEDGE

THE FOLLOWING TEST IS TO DETERMINE A churchgoer's knowledge of the Holy Bible. A person taking this test should not use the Bible or any technological devices to find answers.

1. The first five books of the Old Testament (OT) are known as the _____ or _____ _____.
2. The OT was first written in these two languages _____ and _____.
3. There are _____ books in the OT.
4. The OT consists of these five categories _____, _____, _____, _____, _____.
5. Ecclesiastes and Song of Songs were written by _____.
6. The four OT Major Prophets are_____, _____, _____, and _____.
7. There are _____ OT Minor Prophets.
8. The first king of Israel was _____.
9. The second and third kings of Israel were _____ and _____.
10. The wisest man in the OT was _____.
11. _____ led the Israelites out of Egypt.

12. The sons of _____ or _____ represent the twelve tribes of Israel.
13. The first book in the OT is _____.
14. The first book in the New Testament (NT) is _____.
15. The last book in the NT is _____.
16. There are _____ books in the NT.
17. The NT was first written in this language _____.
18. The writers of the first four books of the NT are _____, _____, _____, and _____.
19. Of the writers of the first four books in the NT, which of these two were not Jesus' apostles? _____ and _____.
20. Jesus chose twelve men as his apostles. Name at least six of these men. _____, _____, _____, _____, and _____.
21. The apostle who betrayed Jesus was _____ _____.
22. The Christian era began with the _____ of _____.
23. The genealogy of Jesus is found in these two NT books: _____ and _____.
24. The apostle who wrote nearly half of NT books was _____.
25. Two of Jesus' half-brothers wrote these books: _____ and _____.
26. Jesus was baptized in the _____ River by _____ the _____.
27. This apostle denied knowing Jesus after Jesus' arrest _____.
28. This apostle had doubts about Jesus' resurrection. _____.

29. This apostle, not specifically identified in the Bible, is believed to be the one which Jesus loved the most. _____.

30. This short man climbed a tree in order to see Jesus. _____.

31. Jesus raised this man who had been dead for four days. _____.

32. Jesus appeared before this Roman governor before being crucified: _____.

33. Jesus was crucified on this day of the week. _____

34. Jesus was in the tomb for _____ _____.

35. Jesus was raised from the dead on this day of the week. _____

36. After his resurrection, Jesus appeared to his disciples for _____ days.

37. These three apostles belonged to Jesus' inner circle _____, _____ and _____

38. Jesus died for _____ sins.

✛ GRADING:

Correct answers to 34 or more questions: Excellent
Correct answers to at least 28 questions: Good
Correct answers to 20 questions: Fair
Correct answers to 12 questions or less: Poor

Members who have been on a church roll for five or more years should be more knowledgeable of the Bible than those who have less than five years as members.

The primary purpose of this quiz is to determine whether the Bible is being taught in churches or in the home. Through the teaching, preaching or the reading of God's Word at church or in the home, a biblical knowledge is attained. The reading or hearing about the Bible may not bring about knowledge. The study of the Word should.

✢ ANSWERS TO THE QUIZ:

1. Pentateuch or The Law
2. Hebrew and Aramaic
3. 39
4. The Law. History. Poetic. Major Prophets. Minor Prophets.
5. Solomon
6. Isaiah, Jeremiah, Ezekiel, Daniel
7. 12
8. Saul
9. David and Solomon
10. Solomon
11. God
12. Jacob or Israel
13. Genesis
14. Matthew
15. Revelation
16. 27
17. Greek
18. Matthew, Mark, Luke and John
19. Mark and Luke
20. Matthew, John, Peter (or Simon), Andrew, James, Philip, Thomas, Bartholomew, James (son of Alphaeus), Thaddaeus (aka Judas), Simon (the zealot) and Judas Iscariot. (any six of these twelve).
21. Judas Iscariot
22. Birth of Jesus
23. Matthew and Luke
24. Paul
25. James and Jude

26. Jordan and John the Baptist
27. Peter
28. Thomas
29. John
30. Zacchaeus
31. Lazarus
32. Pilate
33. Friday
34. 3
35. Sunday
36. 40
37. Peter, James, John
38. Everyone's

CHAPTER FORTY

WHAT GOD HAS SAID TO HIS PEOPLE

✝ OLD TESTAMENT

GOD SPOKE TO HIS CHOSEN PEOPLE CENTURIES AGO when He spoke through the prophet Jeremiah to the southern Kingdom of Judah.

The ten tribes of the Northern Kingdom of Israel had been overthrown in 722 B.C by Assyria. God now had a message for the two tribes remaining in the Southern Kingdom: the same fate would befall them if they didn't forsake their sins and disobedience to Him. Their refusal to turn back to God led to their captivity by Babylon in 587 B.C., and to the destruction of the magnificent temple which had been built during the reign of Solomon.

When captured by the Assyrians, the Northern Kingdom of Israel, was dispersed throughout many regions held by their captor. A mystery remains to this day about the disappearance and whereabouts of these ten tribes.

It is not known how many Jews from the Southern Kingdom of Judah returned to their homeland after 70 years of captivity.

Before the captivity, God spoke to Jeremiah this message which was to be delivered to the Southern Kingdom of Judah:

This is the word that came to Jeremiah from the Lord:

"Listen to the terms of this covenant and tell them to the people of Judah and to those who live in Jerusalem. Tell them that this is what the Lord, the God of Israel, says: 'Cursed is the one who does not obey the terms of this covenant - the terms I commanded your ancestors when I brought them out of Egypt, out of the iron-smelting furnace. I said, 'Obey me and do everything I command you, and you will be my people, and I will be your God. Then I will fulfill the oath I swore to your ancestors, to give a land flowing with milk and honey – the land you possess today."

I answered, "Amen, Lord."

The Lord said to me, "Proclaim all these words in the towns of Judah and in the streets of Jerusalem: 'Listen to the terms of this covenant and follow them. From the time I brought your ancestors up from Egypt until today, I warned them again and again, saying, "Obey me." But they did not listen or pay attention; instead, they followed the stubbornness of their evil hearts. So I brought on them all the curses of the covenant I had commanded them to follow but that they did not keep.

Then the Lord said to me, "There is a conspiracy among the people of Judah and those who live in Jerusalem. They have returned to the sins of their ancestors, who refused to listen to my words. They have followed other gods to serve them. Both Israel and Judah have broken the covenant I made with their ancestors. Therefore, this is what the Lord says: 'I will bring on them a disaster they cannot escape. Although they cry out to me, I will not listen to them. The towns of Judah and the people of Jerusalem will go and cry out to the gods to whom they burn incense, but they will not help them at all when disaster strikes. You, Judah, have as many gods as you have towns; and the altars you have set up to burn incense to that shameful god Baal are as many as the streets of Jerusalem.'

"Do not pray for this people or offer any plea or petition for them, because I will not listen when they call to me in the time of their distress (Jer. 11: 1-14).

God's requirements of His people, from the time of the first covenant until now, remain the same. He expects complete obedience, a turning away from other gods and away from our sinfulness.

Christians have an unchangeable God. His words and teachings are the same. He does not have different standards for each generation. Humans are the ones who determine their lifestyles, customs and cultures. "Jesus Christ is the same yesterday and today and forever" (Heb. 13:8). God has not changed over the centuries. His requirements for this time and age remain the same.

Throughout the pages of the Holy Word, God appointed prophets to deliver messages to His people: messages of doom and coming disasters. Instead, they chose to go their own way instead of His way. Prophets whom The Lord God chose to speak for Him, were killed.

Are Christians hearing messages of doom and coming disasters from today's pulpits? Surely, the Lord God has appointed and chosen ministers to warn the people about what happens when his people turn away for Him. The beautiful temple was destroyed. Today, we have some beautiful churches.

Today, humanity has its opinions and theories about God or if there is a God. He permits humanity to go its own way but has a timeframe when He will bring judgment to the world which He created. Some Bible scholars call attention to the Rapture which will remove all true believers from the coming disaster. This Rapture will be the time when all true believers are taken up into Heaven.

Mankind is going to worship something, whether the imaginations in their own minds or the true God:

> The blacksmith takes a tool and works with it in the coals; he shapes an idol with hammers, he forges it with the might of his arm. He gets hungry and loses his strength; he drinks no water and grows faint. The carpenter measures with a line and makes an outline with a marker; he roughs it out with chisels and marks it with compasses. He shapes it in human form, human form in all its glory, that it may dwell in a shrine. He cut down cedars, or perhaps took a cypress or oak. He let it grow among the trees of the forest, or planted a pine, and the rain made it grow. It is used as fuel for burning; some of it he takes and warms himself, he kindles a fire and bakes bread. But he also fashions a god and worships it; he makes an idol and bows down to it. Half of the wood he burns in the fire; over it he prepares his meal, he roasts his meat and eats his fill. He also warms himself and says, "Ah! I am warm; I see the fire." From the rest he makes a god, his idol; he bows down to it and worships. He prays to it and says, "Save me! You are my god!" They know nothing, they understand nothing; their eyes are plastered over so they cannot see, and their minds closed so they cannot understand. No one stops to think, no one has the knowledge or understanding to say, "Half of it I used for fuel; I even baked bread over its coals, I roasted meat and I ate. Shall I make a detestable thing from what is left? Shall I bow down to a block of wood?" Such a person feeds on ashes; a deluded heart misleads him; he cannot

save himself, or say "Is not this thing in my right hand a lie?" (Isaiah 44: 12-20).

The world's population today is not carving out pieces of wood for their gods, but by their choices, have shaped gods which fit their desires. Instead of pieces of wood there is the thirst for money, power, authority, fame, luxuries, gadgets, experiences and many other things.

✣ NEW TESTAMENT

Jesus predicted the destruction of Jerusalem and its beautiful temple:

> "Jesus left the temple and was walking away when his disciples came up to him to call his attention to its buildings. "Do you see all these things?" he asked. "Truly I tell you, not one stone here will be left on another; everyone will be thrown down" (Matt. 24: 1-2).

In these two verses, Jesus predicted the destruction of the Temple. The temple which Solomon had built had been destroyed centuries ago. The temple had been rebuilt, and some say it was more beautiful than the previous one. Jesus' prediction of the destruction of the beautiful temple came true in AD 70.

Religion had reached a low point in Jerusalem when Jesus walked on this earth. A religious party called the Sadducees had replaced the worship of God within the Temple and implanted an institution for profit. Prior to this conversation with his disciples, Jesus had driven from the temple those using it as a money-making source. Politics and outside interests were placed inside the walls of the Temple.

Another religious party, the Pharisees, were dogmatic in their keeping of the Laws of Moses. Their many additions to the laws became an addiction where the Pharisees were worshipping Moses' Law instead of the Lord God.

God speaking from the Holy Bible tells his people that he is a jealous God:

> "You shall not make for yourself an image in the form of anything in heaven above or on the earth beneath or in the waters below. You shall not bow down to them or worship them; for I, the Lord your God, am a jealous God, punishing the children for the sin of the parents to the third and fourth generation of those who hate me, but showing love to a thousand generations of those who love me and keep my commandments" (Exodus 20: 4-6).

Throughout the pages of the Bible, God gives his warnings and encouragements. The hearts of humans have become hardened, and there is a continual drifting away from His ways. Humanity becomes like a life raft without a motor or paddle. It drifts out-to-sea, further away from the shore and gets or ends up lost.

Today's Christian church has lost its way. There is very little spirituality. Jesus made it very clear to the church at Ephesus:

> "Yet I hold this against you: You have forsaken the love you had at first. Consider how far you have fallen! Repent and do the things which you did at first. If you do not repent, I will come to you and remove your lampstand from its place" (Rev. 2: 4-5).

Ears should be listening, and eyes should be seeing what is happening in churches throughout America. Condoning non-Christian practices by those confessing Christianity goes unchecked.

There are many warnings throughout the Bible of God's impending judgement upon those who disobey and continue in their sinfulness.

The last book of the Holy Bible contains another warning by Jesus to the Church at Laodicea: I know your deeds, that you are neither cold nor hot. I wish you were either one or the other! So, because you are lukewarm - neither hot nor cold - I am about to spit you out of my mouth" (Rev. 3:15-16).

God is explicit with his warnings of judgment on those who claim the Name of the Lord Jesus and are disobedient in carrying out His purpose.

CONCLUSION

MULTITUDES WILL DISAGREE WITH MY WRITINGS. FROM the creation, and through the days of Jesus, biblical prophecies have fallen on deaf ears. I'm not a prophet or a predictor of the future. I do believe, however, that God's patience is running thin, and that my inspiration for writing this was from God.

Here are some questions to ponder:

> Is your church more spiritual today than it was a year ago?

> Is your church advancing or declining in membership?

> How about you? Are you growing and more spiritual today than you were one year ago?

There will never be any perfect churches for there aren't any perfect people. Seekers who go looking for a Utopia will never find one. I am neither an optimist nor a pessimist. The goal of every Christian is to become like Jesus.

I have tried not to be too critical of churches with their programs and their means of worship. Denominational churches throughout America mostly function in ways similar with other churches in their denomination. Some are liberal, some are very conservative, and some are in between. Churches practice ways which are the same within other churches throughout America. It's not just churches in your area which are closings their doors. It's everywhere.

The Christianity being practiced today in the 21st Century by various denominational groups and the Roman Catholic Church would not be recognizable by followers of Jesus in the 1st Century. The New Testament writers described a different type of Christianity from the one which we are practicing in our churches and in our lives.

I have tried to give a bird's eye view of what is happening in various denominations and in the Roman Catholic Church.

Parishioners appear to be content with their present modes of worship and believe that this is what Christianity is about. Church members don't know enough about the words being preached from the pulpit to discern whether they are hearing God's message or not.

Within the Christian church, trends and movements have found fertile grounds. These trends and movements will destroy the present biblical practices of Christianity and lead to churches shuttering their windows and doors and the demise of Christianity in America.

I have come down heavy on spiritual leaders, pastors and ministers. It could be because I am a pastor and a minister of God. Without doubt, many of these men of the cloth are the number one cause of **THE KILLING OF THE CHRISTIAN CHURCH IN AMERICA.** I have personally experienced, been acquainted with, rubbed elbows, sat under, and heard them in many churches. The decay and decline come from what is being taught by false and ungodly men who are vocationally oriented and who are standing in the pulpit for a paycheck.

During the next thirty-one years the following will happen:

> Churches will continue with the closing of their doors. Rural churches will be the first to close. Then churches in small towns next, followed by suburban churches and then lastly, larger downtown churches in populated cities.
>
> More and more church members within these churches will go from church to church trying to

find a church which practices Christian values and beliefs.

Baptisms and church membership will continue their numerical downward spiral.

More pulpits, teachers and leadership positions will be filled by those who are not God called.

The elderly will fade into the sunset and will not be replaced by millennials.

State and federal regulations will interfere and stop the spread of Christian values. Politicians from other religious groups and cults will be elected to high government offices and promote their ungodly beliefs.

"In God We Trust" will be removed from our greenbacks and coins.

Churches will depart from any evangelistic efforts and continue their move to socially oriented programs.

The lifestyles of Christians will become more blatantly unbiblical, leading them to believe that some teachings from the Bible are antiquated.

Approaching the year 2050, Christianity will have lost its influence in America. Other religious groups and cults will be making a greater impact in the lives of Americans.

As mentioned previously, some of these trends and their effects on the Church are greater than others:

Members who have very little knowledge of the Bible.

Teachers who don't practice or believe that all Scripture is God breathed.

Ministers who are not God called.

Those who maintain that Christianity is about love without judgment.

Those churches without evangelistic efforts.

Churches which exist for the purpose of social functions only.

Things outside the church which are making and will make the most impact include:

The teaching within colleges and universities by liberal and atheistic professors.

The media, television and Hollywood.

The policies by federal, state and local governments of what is constitutionally permitted for Christian churches.

The lack of interest in Christianity by Millennials.

The use of Christian churches by political parties to obtain their goals.

It takes only one person or an atheist to protest a religious practice and start the ball moving against the godly.

✢ PEOPLE AND THEIR VALUES/A MORAL DECLINE

On October 23, 2019, there appeared in the Rocky Mount (NC) Telegram the article "America Must Address Its Moral Decline" by Walter E. Williams who is a professor of economics at George Mason University. The purpose of Professor Williams' article was to answer the questions of whether it is moral and just for one person to be forcibly used to serve the purposes of another and, if that person does not peaceably submit to such use, should force be initiated against him. Basically, Mr. Williams' writing was about the U.S. Congress' legislation to take taxpayers dollars to pay for the bills of others. Here are some excerpts from his article:

> "Last week, U. S. Attorney General William Barr told A University of Notre Dame Law School audience the attacks on religious liberty have contributed to a moral decline that's in part manifested by increases in suicides, mental illness and drug attrition. Barr said that our moral decline is not random but 'organized destruction.' Namely that 'Secularists and their allies have marshaled all the forces of mass communication, popular culture, the entertainment industry and academia in an unremitting assault on religion and traditional values.'

> The attorney general is absolutely correct. Whether we have the stomach to own up to it or not, we have become an immoral people left with little more than the pretense of morality. The left's attack on religion is just the tiny tip of the iceberg in our nations' moral decline."

It didn't just happen. Morality practices of Christians in and out of the church have been on the decline in America's churches for decades. The inroads and trends mentioned in this writing will become more dominant as other enemies of the church develop.

God will finally intervene and put an end to any pretense of being His people.

✢ SOME CONCLUDING PREDICTIONS

God will allow and permit these trends and inroads to continue their destructive paths. He is a jealous God. Through His Word and His Holy Spirit, He calls people to repentance and to faith in Him.

God as he did in his eternal plan and time with the Israelites, will bring any Christianity in churches in America to an end. Only the invisible church without wood, brick and mortar will remain.

Whether through the Rapture or other means, the time is closer today than it was yesterday.

God waits for Christian churches to do His will.

Printed in the United States
By Bookmasters